The Early American Cookbook

The Early American Cookbook

Based on the Alan Landsburg television series *The American Idea*

by Hyla O'Connor

Illustrations by Joan Blume

A Rutledge Book
Prentice-Hall

The facsimile recipes printed here are from:
Susannah Carter, *The Frugal Housewife*
Hannah Glasse, *The Art of Cookery Made Plain and Easy*
Amelia Simmons, *American Cookery*

Courtesy of The Library of Congress
Washington, D.C.

Katherine Pirrott's Receipt Book, Containing Cookery, Physick & Preserving

Courtesy of Pequot Library
Southport, Connecticut

The illustrations in this book are by Joan Blume, who specializes in draw-
ings and paintings of food and cooking utensils. The pictures here are the
results of Ms. Blume's visits to Old Sturbridge Village, Colonial Williamsburg, and the Smithsonian Institution, which has a large collection of the
tools and utensils of colonial times.

ISBN: 0-13-222760-6
Library of Congress Catalog Card Number: 74-76863
Copyright © 1974 by Alan Landsburg Productions, Inc.
All rights reserved, including the right of reproduction in whole or in part
Prepared and produced by The Ridge Press, Inc.—Rutledge
  Books Division, 25 West 43 Street, New York, N.Y. 10036
Published in 1974 by Prentice-Hall, Inc., Englewood Cliffs, N.J.
Printed in the United States of America

The Early American Cookbook

Contents ⤴

Food and Cooking in Colonial America

From the time it was first discovered, America has been considered a land of plenty, and so it has been. Throughout our years as a people, Americans have eaten extremely well, enjoying a rich and varied diet. For this we have to thank the bounteous generosity of our land, the cultural contributions of many nations—not the least of whom are the Indians—and the remarkable ingenuity of our cooks. Working at first under extremely difficult conditions, with limited means and often limited foodstuffs, our earliest cooks—colonial women—created a distinctly American cuisine. The following chapters display their achievements, from the simple to the elegant, always hearty and satisfying—a way of cooking and eating as typically American as the political ideals also fashioned in colonial years, and one that has endured as long.

We may think of this wonderful achievement as surprising, for the earliest settlers in the seventeenth century were remarkably ill prepared for life in the New World. Back at home they had been farmers or towns-folk, or gentlemen in the case of the Virginia settlers. They raised their own food on old, well-established farms, or bought it at local markets; the southern settlers, gentry, had been cared for by servants. None of these people knew anything about surviving in the wilderness. Imagine their arrival in an unknown land, their food supply depleted by the long journey, with no homes awaiting them, no markets, and no time to grow the urgently needed crops! Yet they survived, and in time came to thrive, thanks to their ingenuity, the new foods they discovered and the generous help of the Indians.

The ingenuity colonial women applied to their cooking was a necessity. These were hard-working women, with many other daily tasks to perform besides preparing meals, and the means they had to cook with were limited.

Throughout the colonial period, the variety of foods available to people of average means was often limited in comparison to today, particularly in the North, where the climate was harsher, the soil thinner, and the average person poorer than in the South. Difficulties in preserving food and in transporting it to different regions also limited the variety in any one area. Then, too, there were none of the convenience foods we have today. And the colonial kitchen was a far cry from the modern American kitchen, with its ample supply of automatic cooking tools. But colonial cooks became adept at finding many different ways to prepare the basic foodstuffs, using all the means available—boiling, baking, and stewing— and a liberal addition of spices, to create meals with interest and flavor.

Many of the new dishes these cooks developed were based on what they had learned from the Indians. In fact, without the help of the Indians, the first colonists might have starved to death—many of those in the Jamestown, Virginia, settlement actually did. At first the settlers brought little livestock with them; they did not know how to catch or gather wild foods; and the grain they imported did not grow well in the new climate. So they were dependent on the food the Indians could give them and on the native crops the Indians could teach them to grow.

Perhaps the Indians' greatest gift to the settlers was the knowledge of corn. Grown easily, requiring little care, corn was a major ingredient of the Indians' diet. It quickly became a basic in the diet of the settlers too, and remained so for over a hundred years until it was displaced by wheat.

The Indians taught the settlers not only how to plant and fertilize their corn, but also how to prepare it, and colonial housewives soon added their own recipes. This corn was not the tender, sweet kind we eat today—that was known only among a small Indian tribe in upper New York State and was not discovered by the colonists until the end of the colonial period. The corn the colonists ate was a tougher, starchier kind, which we still call Indian corn. Indian corn came in many colors, and individual tribes each developed their own strain. It is said that you could tell the tribe a person belonged to by the color of the corn he ate. This corn lent itself less well to cooking whole—as in the Indian dish succotash—than to grinding: either coarsely, as in hominy grits, or finely, for the cornmeal used in puddings, breads, and many types of porridge. In the South people liked white cornmeal, while in the North yellow, water-ground cornmeal was preferred. Going under the names suppawn, hasty pudding, or mush, cornmeal porridge, often liberally spiced, was for many seventeenth-century Americans the sole dish eaten at both breakfast and supper.

The Indians also taught the settlers how to grow the native American beans. Green beans, limas, kidney beans, black-eyed peas for the southern Hopping John, pea beans for the New England baked dishes, were all the gift of the Indians and joined corn as sources of hearty nourishment in pre-Revolutionary days. In addition, there were pumpkins, sweet potatoes, and squashes of several varieties. After the first years, the colonists were able to raise the common European vegetables—carrots, cabbage, turnips, and various greens—which they grew from imported seeds. Root vegetables were the most popular simply because they could be stored for the winter. There are not any colonial recipes for fresh greens or salads, since such vegetables were available only during the growing season—unlike today when we can buy them all year round.

In the South, the most popular grain, after about 1700, was rice. Rice first came to America in the late 1600s, according to one story, aboard a ship hailing from Madagascar. Bound for England, the ship was blown off course by a storm and was forced to land at Charleston, South Carolina, for repairs. The captain of the ship, in gratitude for the care he received, gave the governor of the colony a handful of rice grains. The grains were planted, the plants flourished, and rice soon became a major ingredient in the southern diet. It was exported to the North as well.

Besides cultivated crops, there was plenty of wild food to be had for the taking—once the settlers learned how to take it. The northern and southern waters teemed with fish and shellfish. In 1608 Chesapeake Bay reportedly was so thick with fish that Captain John Smith's boat could barely get through. But fish was of little use at first because the settlers, being land-lubbers (and, in the South, gentlemen) had failed to bring along nets, or even the proper hooks and line. Smith's men tried to catch fish with a frying pan—but, not surprisingly, they had little luck. Clams, oysters, and mussels, however, were easily dug. Clams, in fact, sustained the Massachusetts Pilgrims through their first winter, and thus earned the name "Pilgrim bread."

However, since all colonial settlements were on or near the water, people throughout the colonies consumed a great deal of fish once they got the proper equipment—they did so in much greater variety, in fact, than we do today. Scrod, bluefish, and halibut are still commonly eaten. In addition, there were sturgeon, shad, herring, rockfish, catfish, whiting, perch, and bass, all more plentiful then than now. There was plenty of lobster in the North, and crab in the South, and other shellfish as well. Eels and turtles were also popular. By far the most abundant fish was the cod, a New England staple. Codfish certainly put the ingenuity of colonial cooks to the test. They dried and salted it for the winter, and came through with an almost unlimited number of ways to prepare it.

Unskilled at first, the settlers learned to be good marksmen in the woods and fields. There was plenty of wild game, both large and small, to supplement the diet of fish, beans, and corn. Besides deer, elk, hare, and rabbit, there were possums, raccoons, red and gray squirrels, and bear—most of them little eaten today. Bear meat was said to have a taste "very mild and sweet," and in the wilderness its oil was often used for cooking. The average colonist, like the average European, did not eat much domestically raised meat. Cows were valued less for their meat than for their milk, and the butter and cheese that could be made from it. Beef was eaten only when the cows had outlived their usefulness—which explains the predominance of recipes calling for stewing it. Sheep were kept live too, for their yearly supply of wool, and chickens for their eggs. Recipes for chickens were numerous but all call for the long slow cooking that tenderizes the meat. Pigs were the easiest livestock to raise for meat, and in the South pork became a staple. The pigs were allowed to roam at will, and thrived on wild berries, nuts, and roots. Their flesh was thus lean and firm, establishing the type that persists to this day. The origin of Smithfield hams, for which Virginia is still famous, can be traced to the hogs imported from England that were allowed to roam the unfenced Jamestown settlement.

Wild fowl were easy to obtain. In those years, and well into the nineteenth century, they filled the air and crowded the seashores in unbelievable numbers. Songbirds of every kind were hunted for food, along with wild ducks and geese, and shore birds such as plover and curlew. Passenger pigeons were so plentiful that you could catch them by knocking them on the head with a stick as they roosted, or by shooting almost randomly at an air-borne flock. The best-known and perhaps best-loved American bird was the wild turkey, whose domesticated descendant is still a popular favorite. It reportedly weighed as much as fifty pounds and could be found in great numbers everywhere. During the Continental Congress, Benjamin Franklin led a group of lobbyists who wanted the turkey declared the national bird. They lost out to the arguments of those who felt the bird was not sufficiently dignified to be a national symbol. Unfortunately many of the other birds, which were not domesticated, were drastically overhunted. The passenger pigeon became extinct by the early years of the present century; other wild species are now protected by law, and we no longer eat them.

And then there were wild fruits. By the end of spring, and on through the summer and fall, the woods and fields teemed with nuts and berries that the colonists could gather. Blueberries and cranberries were abundant in the North; farther south, wild oranges and persimmons flourished. The colonists planted fruit trees in the earliest years of their settlement, and apples quickly established a dominant position among cultivated fruits. They grew well and stored well, either whole in cold cellars, or dried—or preserved as cider. Wild or cultivated, probably the favorite use for fruits was in desserts, which—judging from the large number of surviving recipes—colonial Americans loved as much as we do today. Peaches grew well in the southern colonies, where a favorite way of preserving them was to pack them in brandy. Elderberries, raspberries, cherries, and all kinds of other fruits were also used for making wines and cordials. The fruits that were not used immediately were strung and hung before the fireplace to dry, for later use.

Throughout the colonial period the preparation of meals was not the relatively simple matter it is today. At the very beginning the settlers undoubtedly used methods developed by the Indians, which survive in certain traditional meals today: the clambake, an ancient, possibly prehistoric, form of cooking in which the food is cooked in a pit that has been dug in the ground and filled with hot stones; and the barbecue, in which food is cooked outdoors on a rack built above an open fire. Once their houses were built, colonial cooks of every rank cooked in the kitchen fireplace. (Cookstoves were not commonly used until the mid-1800s.) Fireplaces were huge affairs. In the smaller homes of the seventeenth century, they sometimes took up an entire wall of the one- or two-room dwelling, and served both to feed the family and to warm it.

Cooking implements were cumbersome, the major one being a large, heavy iron pot that stood on legs before the fire. A later improvement was a type of crane on which the pot could be raised or lowered, permitting the amount of heat to be controlled—which modern cooks now do by turning a knob or pressing a button. Slow cooking, either stewing or baking, was the most common method. Skillets for frying did exist, with handles lengthy enough to keep the long-skirted cook from approaching

the fire too closely, but they were both difficult and dangerous to use. Roasting a piece of meat required constant turning of the spit on which it was skewered, a task often given to children. The colonial housewife had many duties besides that of cook, and stewing was the form of cookery requiring the least attention: you just put everything in the pot, placed it over the fire, and went about your other business, returning occasionally to stir. For baking, cooks used the dutch oven, built into the sides of the fireplace. To warm the oven, they built a fire right inside it; when the fire died down, they cleared out the ashes, put the food in, and sealed the opening with clay. The food—bread or beans, pies or puddings—was simply left in the oven all day, or overnight, until it was done. Baking was made easier in the eighteenth century with the introduction of the "roasting kitchen," a box with one open side, which was set in front of the fire.

Slow cooking, such as baking or stewing, was also favored because it was the best way to tenderize tough meat. And food *had* to be tender; since dentists were virtually nonexistent, and no one knew much about nutrition, most grownups did not have a full set of teeth to chew with. (Milk was not a popular drink, and women who bore many children commonly accepted the saying, "A tooth for every child.") Stews were prepared by cutting the ingredients into small pieces, for ease in serving as well as chewing. Eating utensils as well as teeth were in short supply. As late as 1750, the average home did not possess as much as one table knife for each person—a single hunting knife might be used to prepare the food. Forks too were rare. An elegant gift among the wealthy was a velvet-lined box containing one fork and one knife. The poor still ate with their fingers or dished out their food with wooden spoons from the large cook pot placed on the center of the table—hence the term "spoon meat." The grownups sat on benches at table, the children often standing behind. One trencher—a shallow wooden bowl used as a plate—did duty for two people; a young couple announced their wedding engagement by sharing a trencher.

By 1700 most Americans had risen above the subsistence level, and their meals became more elaborate and varied. Until long after the Revolution 90 percent of the American population lived in rural areas, but land was fertile and provided a relatively comfortable living for those days, though arduous in comparison to modern life. The small urban population thrived on an active trade, both domestic and international, and in the South plantation owners lived in luxury, though their slaves did not. A tradition of hospitality was firmly established in Virginia by the early 1700s. One traveler to that colony wrote: "All over the colony, a universal hospitality reigns; full tables and open doors, the kind salute . . . their manner of living is quite generous and open." Well-to-do Southerners constantly entertained guests, at any time of day and at any meal. Dinner, served at two or three in the afternoon, was the most important meal. It included, for those who could afford such lavishness, several large cuts of meat, game birds, seafood dishes, and meat casseroles, plus vegetables and a variety of desserts.

As the decade of the Revolution approached, the table in a home of moderate means in North or South was laid with pewter. Wealthy city folk and plantation owners dined more elegantly, on damask cloths from serving pieces fashioned of silver by native and European artisans. Wealthy Southerners enjoyed imported French wines with their dinner; elsewhere beer, rum, and hard cider were favored. In fact, throughout the colonial period, Americans of all ages consumed large amounts of strong drink, in addition to coffee, tea, and chocolate. Plain water was scorned, and rightly so, as wells and pumps were often located near open sewers or garbage dumps. Liquor was needed to warm the bodies and raise the spirits of a hard-working people; moreover, it was thought to have medicinal properties—as an aid in warding off fevers, for instance, or, in the case of beer, in preventing scurvy.

Country establishments were largely self-sustaining. On the farm the only purchased provisions were vital ones: salt, spices, and molasses, in addition to rum. Molasses was the predominant sweetener except in wealthy homes, for sugar was very expensive. Salt was used not only for flavoring but for preserving foods, in an age that lacked mechanical refrigerators. Ice houses were not common in the eighteenth century, though cold springs and brooks were used for short-term storage, and less perishable foods such as apples and root vegetables could be kept for months in cold cellars. The traditional method of keeping meat and fish for long periods of time was to salt and dry them, or to pickle them in salt brine—which explains the prevalence of New England salt cod and the boiled dinner made from corned (or pickled) beef. Smoking was another method. Fruits and herbs could be hung before the fireplace to dry. Spices, the search for which first led to the exploration of the New World, were also useful in preservation, and they were urgently needed to disguise the flavor of rotting foods when preservation failed. Few people could afford to discard anything remotely edible; not understanding the connection between rotted food and illness, they ate everything.

Cookbooks of this time often included instructions for making "tainted" food palatable. However, cookbooks were not in common use. Many people were illiterate, printed books were expensive, and in any case, except for the Bible and farmers' manuals, book rarely reached outlying rural areas. We know of only a handful of printed colonial cookbooks, though the later ones were reissued a number of times. Probably none was printed in America before 1742, and even then, when William Parks in Williamsburg pub-

lished *The Compleat Housewife,* it was merely a reprinted version of a book written in England, by Eliza Smith. Like others printed in America before 1776, it completely ignored such staple American ingredients as cornmeal.

Not until 1796 did an American, Amelia Simmons, write a cookbook for American cooks. Appropriately, it was titled *American Cookery,* and it is the first printed record of such American specialties as Indian pudding, johnnycakes, and pickled watermelon rind. It's likely that the author did not invent her recipes for the book—such was not the purpose of cookbooks then—for many of the recipes exist in unpublished form. Cooks not content to pass on their favorite recipes by word of mouth would record them in notebooks, which were handed down for generations from mother to daughter. These recipes were not written in the precise language with which cooks are familiar today, since exact measurements and cooking times did not become standard in cookbooks until after 1900.

In the chapters that follow, you will find recipes typical of the food eaten throughout the original thirteen colonies. Many of them come from the period after 1700, when life had become easier and cooks had the time and means to prepare more complicated dishes—and to write them down. But many of the dishes, such as hasty pudding, had been popular since the time of the earliest settlements.

All the traditional dishes are here, including regional favorites and specialties. The recipes have been adapted for the modern cook from both printed and handwritten sources of the colonial period. Precise measurements, oven temperatures, and cooking times have been added for modern convenience, but in all cases the traditional cooking methods have been followed, and only the ingredients available to colonial cooks have been used. Though sometimes in a different form—packaged baking soda instead of homemade potash, and packaged instead of homemade yeast—these are ingredients readily available today. With them today's cook will be able to recreate the delicious meals our colonial forebears first enjoyed.

MIMI KOREN

I
Soups, Stews, and Chowders

Chowder is an American tradition—and the original one-dish dinner, as much a boon to the early American cook as to her modern counterpart. These hearty dishes will warm the hungry diner, as welcome beginnings to any meal or as meals in themselves. The big black iron stewpot, set on the coals or hung over the fire on a crane, was the most essential of the colonial woman's kitchen utensils. In it a soup, a stew, or a chowder could be made that would serve as the main dish of several meals. Sometimes the meat, fish, or fowl that had served to give the mixture its flavor would be the center of one meal, with the broth and whatever vegetables had been cooked with it waiting to serve as tomorrow's dinner, perhaps with the addition of today's leftovers.

Hearty Beef Soup

6 servings

¼ cup butter
2 cups shredded potatoes
2 tablespoons chopped onion
1 tablespoon all-purpose flour
4 cups milk

1 package (3½ ounces) dried beef
1 can (8¾ ounces) whole kernel corn
¼ teaspoon celery seed
Salt and pepper to taste

Melt butter in a 3-quart saucepan. Add potatoes, onion, and 1 cup water. Cover and bring to a boil; lower heat and simmer about 15 minutes, or until potatoes are cooked. Stir flour into mixture and simmer 1 minute. Gradually add milk, stirring constantly. Break dried beef into small pieces and stir into mixture with undrained corn and celery seed. Heat, but do not boil. Season to taste with salt and pepper and serve piping hot.

Favorite Oxtail Soup

6 servings

1 oxtail
2 whole cloves
1 teaspoon salt
¼ teaspoon pepper
1 onion, sliced

2 tablespoons butter
1 carrot, sliced
1 small turnip, diced
½ cup chopped celery
1 teaspoon lemon juice

Cut oxtail into pieces and put in a large kettle with cloves, salt, pepper, and 1 quart water. Simmer 2 hours, or until meat is tender. Cool. Strain mixture and remove fat, reserving meat and stock. Sauté onion and oxtail in butter until lightly browned. Return to stock with carrot, turnip, and celery. Simmer about 30 minutes, or until vegetables are tender. Taste and add more seasonings if necessary. Stir in lemon juice and serve.

Note: *Seasonings in oxtail soup can be varied as desired. Some people like to use 2 cups tomato juice as half the liquid. Seasonings such as cinnamon, thyme, marjoram, and bay leaf are sometimes also added; 2 tablespoons of dry sherry stirred into the soup just before serving lends an interesting flavor.*

Philadelphia Pepper Pot

A number of delicious foods from colonial days are attributed to the Quaker City. This savory tripe soup is one. Scrapple is another, although it was the Pennsylvania Dutch who brought it to the Penn colony. Sticky buns, fragrant with cinnamon and rich with the combination of butter, spice, and sugar in which they were laid before baking, are still another.

3 pounds tripe	*1 bay leaf*
1 veal knuckle	*2 sprigs thyme or ½ teaspoon dried*
2 pounds cracked marrow bones	*thyme*
2 large onions, sliced	*1 carrot, cut in chunks*
5 whole cloves	*5 potatoes, diced*
1 teaspoon whole allspice	*2 teaspoons dried marjoram*
½ teaspoon crushed red pepper	*2 tablespoons chopped parsley*
Several sprigs parsley	*Salt and pepper to taste*

Wash tripe; put in a kettle and cover with 4 quarts cold water. Bring to a boil, reduce heat, cover, and simmer 6 to 7 hours, or until tripe is very tender. Remove from heat and cool tripe in broth. When cool, cut into very small pieces. Reserve broth. While tripe is cooking, put veal knuckle in a kettle and cover with 2 quarts water. Remove marrow from marrow bones and heat in a small saucepan. Add onions and cook until tender but not browned. Add to veal bone with remaining marrow bones. Add cloves, allspice, red pepper, parsley, bay leaf, thyme, and carrot. Bring to a boil, reduce heat, cover, and simmer about 5 hours. Remove from heat and let cool. Remove veal bone; chop any meat left on bone and add to chopped tripe. Cool broth and refrigerate meat and both broths overnight. The following day, skim fat from top of broths and remove fat from top of cut-up tripe. Combine the two broths in a large soup kettle with the tripe, veal, potatoes, marjoram, parsley, and salt and pepper to taste. Bring to a boil, reduce heat, cover, and simmer 45 minutes.

Barley Broth   *10 to 12 servings*

3 pounds veal or lamb bones   *1 cup light cream*
1 lamb shank   *½ teaspoon ground mace*
1 cup pearl barley   *½ cup white wine*
¼ cup currants   *1 teaspoon sugar*
¼ cup seedless raisins   *Salt to taste*
2 tablespoons oatmeal

Place bones and shank in a large soup kettle. Cover with water and bring to
a boil. Lower heat, cover, and simmer 30 minutes. Remove from heat and
skim off any scum that has collected on the top of the broth. Add the barley.
Cover and simmer at least 1 hour, or until barley is tender. Add the currants
and the raisins. Stir together the oatmeal and cream and stir into the broth.
Add the mace. Bring to a boil and cook just until the mixture has thickened
a little. Add the wine, sugar, and salt to taste. Simmer gently about 15 minutes. Serve with some of the meat from the lamb shank.

Connecticut Lobster Soup

4 to 6 servings

In colonial days, the Connecticut shores were rich with lobster, there for the taking. This delectable soup is notable for its lovely pale pink color and for its unusual, delicate little dumplings.

1 large cooked lobster	Salt and freshly ground pepper to taste
Yolks of 2 hard-cooked eggs	Pinch of mace
2 teaspoons butter	2 quarts chicken broth
1 egg	

Extract meat from cooked lobster; reserve coral. Cut tail meat into chunks and set aside. Remove meat from claws and chop very fine. Mash together hard-cooked egg yolks and butter. Combine with chopped lobster meat to make a smooth mixture. Add raw egg and mix well. Add salt, pepper, and mace. Form into small balls about the size of a walnut. Set aside. Bring chicken broth to a boil. Add lobster chunks and simmer 5 minutes. Mash coral in a bowl to form a smooth paste. Add a little of the hot chicken broth to thin the consistency. Stir slowly into stock until mixture turns pink. Drop in lobster balls and simmer about 5 minutes, but do not boil. If mixture boils the lobster balls may break up and the soup darken.

Cream of Quahog Soup

6 to 8 servings

24 clams, cooked, or 2 cans	2 tablespoons butter
(7 ounces each) canned clams	2 tablespoons all-purpose flour
½ cup liquor from clams	1 cup heavy cream
2 onions, very thinly sliced	Salt and freshly ground pepper to taste
3 cups milk	Minced parsley
1 teaspoon sugar	

Chop the clams very fine. Place in the top part of a double boiler with the liquor and onion. Cook over direct heat for 5 minutes, or until onion is soft. Add milk and sugar; place over boiling water and heat thoroughly. Blend the butter and flour to make a smooth paste. Stir into clam mixture. Cook 3 minutes, or until mixture thickens slightly. At this point it can be strained and clams and onion discarded, or they can be left in. Stir in cream and season to taste. Heat over hot water until of serving temperature. Serve in soup cups with a sprinkle of parsley.

Note: *The New England coast in colonial days was abundant in clams of many kinds. (Quahog is the settlers' rendition of the Indian word for clam.) Although this and other clam soups may be more authentic made with fresh clams, today's home cook may want to save time and effort—and money, too, in most cases—by using canned clams.*

Clam and Mushroom Bisque   4 servings

½ pound fresh mushrooms   *3 cups clam broth*
3 tablespoons butter   *1 cup cream*
3 tablespoons all-purpose flour *Salt and freshly ground pepper to taste*

Clean and chop mushrooms. Melt butter in a saucepan. Add chopped mushrooms and cook about 3 minutes. Blend in flour and cook 1 minute. Remove from heat and stir in clam broth. Cook, stirring constantly, until mixture thickens slightly. Add cream and seasonings and heat thoroughly, but do not boil.

Cream of Oyster Soup   4 servings

1 pint oysters, with liquor   *1 small bay leaf*
4 cups milk   *¼ cup butter*
1 slice onion   *¼ cup all-purpose flour*
2 stalks celery, chopped   *Salt and freshly ground pepper to taste*
1 sprig parsley

Pick over oysters and remove bits of shell. Chop oysters very fine and combine with liquor. Place in a small saucepan and heat slowly to the boiling point. Set aside. Combine milk with onion, celery, parsley, and bay leaf. Scald milk. Strain, reserving milk and discarding vegetables. Melt butter in a saucepan. Blend in flour and cook 1 minute. Remove from heat. Stir in milk. Cook, stirring constantly, until mixture comes to a boil and thickens slightly. Add oysters and seasonings to taste. Serve piping hot with crisp toast.

Okra Soup   6 servings

2 pounds okra, finely sliced (frozen   *1 cup fresh lima beans*
* may be used)*   *1 sprig or pinch of thyme*
1 tablespoon bacon drippings   *Salt and freshly ground black pepper*
1 tablespoon cider vinegar   * to taste*
1 ham bone   *1½ cups corn, cut from cob*
6 tomatoes, peeled and chopped   *3 cups hot cooked rice*

Cook okra in a skillet with the bacon drippings and vinegar, stirring constantly, until okra loses its slimy consistency. Transfer okra to a large kettle. Add ham bone, tomatoes, beans, and thyme. Season with a little salt and pepper. Bring to a boil and simmer until meat left on bone is very tender. Check consistency, and if soup is too thick, thin with a little water. Remove bone. Remove ham from bone and cut in small pieces; return meat to kettle. Add corn. Cook 3 to 5 minutes, or until corn is tender. Taste and adjust seasonings, if necessary. To serve, put a small mound of hot rice in a deep soup bowl and pour soup over rice.

Note: *The peculiarly "slippery" quality that cooked okra sometimes takes on is liked by some people, but disliked by many more. Treated as it is in this recipe, that objection is overcome, and the full and unusual flavor can be enjoyed.*

Black Bean Soup   6 to 8 servings

2 cups black beans   3 tablespoons butter
2 medium onions, diced   1 tablespoon lemon juice
1 clove garlic   ¼ cup dry sherry
1½ teaspoons salt   1 lemon, thinly sliced
¼ teaspoon pepper   1 hard-cooked egg, minced
¼ teaspoon dry mustard

Pick over beans. Cover with cold water and let soak overnight. Drain well. Add 6 cups water, onion, garlic, salt, and pepper. Bring to a boil, lower heat, and simmer 1 to 2 hours, or until beans are tender. Force mixture through a coarse sieve. Return to saucepan. Stir in mustard, butter, lemon juice, and sherry. Heat, but do not boil. (If mixture is too thick it can be diluted with a little hot water or hot milk.) Serve in soup bowls with a slice of lemon and a little minced egg floating on top of the soup.

Cabbage Soup   6 servings

Cabbage was one of the vegetables—along with potatoes, carrots, parsnips— that could be "put by" in cold cellars for later use. On a winter day, cabbage soup was particularly welcome in a season when few vegetables were available.

1 small head cabbage   1 cup cream
3 cups milk   Salt and freshly ground pepper to taste

Chop cabbage very fine. It should measure about 3 cups. Cover with water in a saucepan; bring to a boil, lower heat, and simmer until tender. Drain water from cabbage; reserve 1 cup of the liquid and combine with cabbage. Add milk, cream, salt, and pepper. Heat thoroughly, but do not boil.

Old-Fashioned Split Pea Soup   8 servings

2 cups yellow split peas   1 ham bone
1 onion, sliced   Salt and pepper to taste

Pick over peas. Cover with cold water and let soak overnight. Drain well and place in a large soup kettle. Add onion, ham bone, and 3 quarts water. Bring to a boil, reduce heat, and simmer 3 to 4 hours, or until peas are very soft. Remove ham bone and put peas through a sieve. Return to pot and season to taste. If soup is too thick, add a little boiling water.

Purée of Split Pea Soup

10 to 12 servings

1 cup yellow split peas
1½ cups green split peas
¼ pound salt pork
¼ cup chopped cooked ham
2 stalks celery, diced
1 carrot, sliced
1 onion, thinly sliced

¼ teaspoon pepper
1 clove garlic, minced
3 tablespoons all-purpose flour
3 medium potatoes, peeled and thinly sliced
1½ cups light cream, scalded

Pick over peas. Cover with water and let soak overnight. Drain and place in a large kettle. Add 4 quarts of cold water. Bring to a boil, lower heat, and simmer 30 minutes. Cut salt pork in small pieces. Sauté in a heavy skillet until some of the fat has cooked out. Add ham, celery, carrot, onion, pepper, and garlic and sauté a few minutes. Add flour and cook 5 minutes, stirring. Scrape vegetable mixture into pot with the peas. Add potatoes and simmer 2 hours until everything is tender. Rub mixture through a sieve. Return to pot and taste for seasoning. Stir in cream and heat, but do not boil. If purée is too thick, add boiling water to make it of serving consistency.

Country Baked Soup

6 servings

1 cup dried split peas
1 pound boneless lamb, cut in cubes
1 carrot, diced

1 onion, minced
1 teaspoon salt
Generous grind of pepper

Pick over peas. Cover with cold water and let soak overnight. Preheat oven to 300°. Drain peas and place in a bean pot. Add remaining ingredients and stir lightly. Add enough cold water to cover mixture entirely. Cover and bake 3 to 4 hours, or until mixture is well cooked. Add boiling water during cooking if soup becomes too thick.

Celery Soup

4 servings

2 cups thinly sliced celery
2 thick slices onion
2 cups milk
Generous shake of ground mace

¼ cup butter
2 tablespoons all-purpose flour
1½ teaspoons salt
Dash of cayenne

Place celery and 3 cups water in a saucepan. Simmer 20 minutes, or until celery is tender. Reserve. Combine onion, milk, and mace and simmer 20 minutes. Melt butter in a saucepan. Stir in flour and salt and cook 1 minute. Remove from heat. Strain milk mixture and discard onions. Stir milk into flour-butter mixture. Cook, stirring constantly, until smooth and thickened. Add celery and the water in which it was cooked and heat thoroughly. Stir in cayenne and serve piping hot.

Nantucket Cucumber Soup

4 to 6 servings

3 potatoes, peeled and cubed
2 leeks, white part only, thoroughly
washed and sliced
1 sprig parsley
1 teaspoon salt
½ teaspoon pepper

½ cup butter
2 onions, finely chopped
2 cups light cream
1 large cucumber, peeled and finely
chopped

Place potatoes, leeks, parsley, salt, pepper, and 1 quart water in a large saucepan. Cover and simmer gently about 1 hour, or until vegetables are very well done. Melt butter in a skillet. Add onion and cook until soft but not browned. Combine onion with cooked potato mixture and put through a sieve. Cool thoroughly. When mixture is cold, stir in cream and chopped cucumber. Serve well chilled.

Potato Soup

6 servings

4 cups diced potatoes
2 medium onions, minced
2 tablespoons butter
1 tablespoon all-purpose flour
4 cups milk

1 teaspoon salt
⅛ teaspoon pepper
Dash of ground nutmeg
Minced parsley or chives

Combine potatoes and onion with enough water to cover and cook until tender. Force mixture, including the liquid, through a sieve. Melt butter in a large saucepan. Stir in flour and cook 1 minute. Remove from heat and stir in milk, salt, pepper, and nutmeg. Return to heat and bring to a boil, stirring. Stir in potato mixture and heat, but do not boil. Add more seasoning if necessary. Serve piping hot, garnished with parsley or chives.

Watercress and Corn Soup

6 to 8 servings

2 teaspoons minced parsley
Pinch of marjoram
1 quart beef stock
2 cups fresh corn cut from the cob, or 1
can (16 ounces) whole kernel corn

½ cup chopped watercress
3 tablespoons butter
Salt and freshly ground pepper to
taste
2 hard-cooked eggs, sliced (optional)

Combine parsley, marjoram, and beef stock in a saucepan. Bring to a boil and simmer 5 minutes. Add corn and simmer 25 minutes, or until corn is well cooked. Force mixture through a sieve. Stir in watercress and butter. Season to taste with salt and pepper. Serve piping hot garnished with egg slices, if desired.

Pumpkin Soup

about 6 servings

Pumpkins were one of the Indians' many gifts to the settlers. The cheery orange vegetables were baked in the ashes, stewed, made into puddings and into the pumpkin pie that has become a Thanksgiving tradition. They were also—less familiar to us now—made into a hearty soup.

1 small pumpkin	Salt and pepper to taste
⅓ cup butter, divided	Pinch of ground allspice
1 quart chicken or beef stock	Milk or light cream
1 tablespoon sugar	

Peel, seed, and cut pumpkin in small chunks. There should be about 1 quart of pumpkin wedges or pieces. Place in a saucepan with half the butter, the stock, sugar, and 1 teaspoon salt. Bring to a boil, lower heat, and simmer about 35 minutes, or until pumpkin is tender. Press through a sieve and return pulp to saucepan. Season with pepper and allspice and additional salt if necessary. Add remaining butter and enough milk to make a soup of the desired consistency. Heat, but do not boil. Serve with fried bread, if desired.

Farmer's Corn Soup

6 servings

12 ears corn	2 egg yolks, well beaten
3 cups rich milk, divided	Dash of sugar
2 tablespoons butter	Dash of ground nutmeg
1 tablespoon all-purpose flour	

Cut kernels off corncobs. Place kernels in a heavy kettle with 1 cup milk; simmer until soft. Add remaining milk. Blend butter with flour. Stir into soup and cook until mixture thickens slightly, stirring constantly. Do not boil. Stir egg yolks slowly into soup. Heat, but do not boil. Serve with a sprinkling of sugar and nutmeg.

Note: *Because of its scarcity and high price, sugar was often used as a seasoning, rather than an ingredient, in Early American times.*

Lobster Stew

4 servings

2 cups cubed cooked lobster meat	1 cup cream, heated
3 tablespoons butter	Salt and freshly ground pepper to
Tomalley (liver) from cooked lobster	taste
1½ cups milk, heated	

Sauté lobster meat in butter for 2 minutes. Add tomalley and blend well. Slowly stir in hot milk and cream. Season to taste with salt and pepper. Heat a little longer, until piping hot, but do not boil. Serve with toasted crackers.

Clam Stew

Clam Stew *8 servings*

½ cup butter
2 tablespoons all-purpose flour
1 quart milk, heated
1 quart shucked clams with liquor, or
  2 cans (7 ounces each) minced clams

Salt and freshly ground pepper to
  taste
2 eggs, well beaten

Melt butter in a large saucepan. Stir in flour and cook about 1 minute, stirring constantly. Remove from heat and stir in warm milk. Cook, stirring constantly, until mixture comes to a boil. Remove from heat. Pick over clams and remove any bits of shell. Drain off liquor and reserve. Chop clams fine. Place liquor in a saucepan, add chopped clams and simmer 3 minutes; or heat canned clams. Combine with milk mixture and heat thoroughly, but do not boil. Season. Place eggs in a tureen; pour heated clam mixture into tureen and stir thoroughly. Serve immediately.

Oyster Stew

Oyster Stew *4 to 6 servings*

1 quart shucked fresh oysters
¼ cup butter
2 cups milk, heated

2 cups cream, heated
1 teaspoon salt
¼ teaspoon pepper

Clean and pick over oysters. Place in a 1½-quart saucepan with butter and cook until edges curl. Gradually stir in milk, cream, salt, and pepper. Heat until piping hot, but do not boil. If a richer stew is desired, add more butter and stir until well blended. Serve with oyster crackers.

Martha's Vineyard Chicken Chowder

Martha's Vineyard Chicken Chowder *10 to 12 servings*

1 5- to 6-pound stewing chicken
¼ pound salt pork, cubed
2 medium onions, sliced
8 cups diced potatoes

1 tablespoon salt
1 quart milk, scalded
2 tablespoons butter

Cut chicken in pieces. Place in a kettle and cover with cold water. Bring to a boil, lower heat, and simmer 2 to 3 hours, or until chicken is tender. Remove from heat and let stand until cool enough to handle. Remove chicken pieces and take all meat from bones. Discard skin and bones. When liquid is cold, remove chicken fat from top of broth. Cut chicken in chunks and return to broth. Sauté salt pork in a skillet until crisp and brown. Remove pieces of pork and sauté onion in fat until soft and lightly browned. Place onion and pork fat in a large kettle; add 1 quart hot water, potatoes, and salt. Bring to a boil and simmer until potatoes are tender. Add chicken and chicken broth. Bring to a boil, and boil 5 to 10 minutes. Add milk and butter and simmer, but do not boil. Serve with common crackers.

Note: *It is easier to cook the chicken one day and prepare the chowder the second day. This method also improves the flavor of the chowder.*

Chicken Chowder

4 servings

2 tablespoons chicken fat
1 onion, sliced
2 stalks celery, minced
2 potatoes, peeled and sliced
1 cup cubed cooked chicken

1 cup hot milk
1 tablespoon all-purpose flour
1 teaspoon salt
⅛ teaspoon pepper

Melt the fat in a heavy saucepan. Add onion and celery and cook until onion is soft but not browned. Add potatoes and 2 cups hot water. Cover and simmer 30 minutes, or until potatoes are tender. Add chicken and hot milk. Mix flour with a little cold water to make a smooth paste. Add to soup mixture, stirring constantly until slightly thickened. Add salt and pepper and serve immediately.

Egg Chowder

6 servings

2 ounces salt pork, diced
5 large potatoes, peeled and thinly
 sliced
2 cups milk, scalded

2 tablespoons butter
Salt and pepper to taste
5 hard-cooked eggs, sliced

Fry salt pork in a saucepan until browned. Add potatoes and enough hot water to cover. Cook 30 minutes, or until potatoes are tender. Add hot milk, butter, salt, and pepper. Heat thoroughly. Just before serving, carefully stir in egg slices. Serve immediately.

Finnan Haddie Chowder

about 4 servings

¼ pound salt pork, cut in ½-inch
 cubes
2 medium onions, sliced
2 large potatoes, peeled and sliced

1 pound finnan haddie fillet
Freshly ground pepper to taste
1 quart milk
Water biscuits

Fry salt pork in a skillet until crisp; remove bits of salt pork and reserve. Cook onion in hot pork fat until lightly browned. Place potatoes in a saucepan and cover with water. Cook 10 minutes. Drain, reserving potato water. Cut fish into 1-inch strips and arrange a layer of fish slices in top part of a large double boiler. Arrange a layer of potato slices over the fish. Sprinkle with pepper and add ½ cup potato water. Add onion and sprinkle with a little pepper. Add milk and cook over simmering water 30 minutes. Place salt pork bits on top of chowder; do not stir. Cover and simmer another 30 minutes. Do not let the water boil, or the soup may curdle. Split, toast, and butter the water biscuits. Serve soup in heated bowls with biscuits.

Note: *Finnan haddie is haddock that has been dried, smoked, and salted; the chowder therefore needs no salt.*

Gloucester Fish Chowder   8 servings

3½ to 4 pounds haddock or cod
1 2-inch cube salt pork
1 medium onion, sliced
4 cups sliced potatoes

1 quart milk, heated
1 tablespoon salt
⅛ teaspoon pepper

Cut fish into chunks and place in a saucepan. Add 2 cups cold water and simmer until fish is tender. Drain, reserving fish and liquid. Cut pork into tiny cubes and cook until light brown and crisp. Remove pork bits with a slotted spoon and reserve. Add onion to fat and cook slowly until tender but not browned. Add fish liquid and potatoes to onion and fat. Add just enough extra water to cover potatoes, if necessary. Cook 30 minutes, or until potatoes are tender. Meanwhile, pick fish from skin and bones, discarding skin and bones. To cooked potato mixture add the fish, hot milk, seasonings, and bits of salt pork. Heat thoroughly, but do not boil. Serve with sour pickles and common crackers.

Note: *It is a custom, and long has been in New England, to serve very hard, large crackers with fish chowders. These are called common crackers, pilot crackers, or water biscuits. Although recipes for the three are not exactly the same, they do have hardness in common. The crackers are split and toasted—and buttered if desired— or just split and put in a tureen; then the chowder is ladled over them. Or each person can crumble or drop crackers into his individual serving.*

Rhode Island Sea Bass Chowder   6 servings

½ cup diced salt pork
4 pounds sea bass
3 strips bacon
4 medium onions, sliced
½ cup chopped parsley

Pinch of summer savory
Boston crackers, split
Butter
2 tablespoons all-purpose flour

Cook the salt pork in a heavy dutch oven until crisp. Cut sea bass into 2-inch cubes. Put a layer of fish over salt pork in bottom of dutch oven. Place a strip of bacon on top. Add some onion. Sprinkle with parsley and a bit of savory. Cover with a layer of split crackers. Repeat layers until all the fish is used. Butter the top layer of crackers. Cover the layers with cold water. Cover kettle and simmer gently about 1 hour, or until fish is cooked. Carefully transfer pieces of fish to a heated tureen. Combine 2 tablespoons of butter with the flour to make a smooth paste. Add to liquid in dutch oven and cook, stirring constantly, until mixture thickens and boils. Pour over fish in tureen. Serve with sour pickles.

Lobster Chowder

8 servings

1 onion, quartered
1 teaspoon dill weed
1 2-pound live lobster
4 cups milk
¼ cup butter

¼ cup cracker meal
2 teaspoons salt
⅛ teaspoon white pepper
¼ teaspoon paprika

Combine onion, dill, and 3 quarts water in a large kettle. Bring to a full boil. Add lobster, head first. Boil gently for 15 minutes, or until lobster is bright red. Remove lobster and set aside. Strain liquid and return to saucepan; bring to a boil. Shell lobster. Add juices and shell to boiling liquid. Boil until liquid is reduced to 2 cups. Strain reduced liquid. Dice lobster meat. Scald milk in a large saucepan. Stir in butter; add reduced liquid, lobster meat, cracker meal, salt, pepper, and paprika. Heat, but do not boil.

Down-East Clam Chowder

6 to 8 servings

1 quart shucked clams with liquor or 2
  cans (7 ounces each) minced clams
2 slices salt pork, cut in cubes
1 onion, sliced
3 medium potatoes, peeled and cut in
  small cubes

3 tablespoons butter
¾ cup milk
¾ cup light cream
1 tablespoon salt
Dash of pepper
6 to 8 large crackers

Pick over clams, removing any bits of shell. Combine clams, liquor, and 3 cups water in a saucepan. Bring to a boil. Drain clams, reserving liquid. Chop the hard portions of the clams and leave the remainder whole, or chop the entire clam, if desired. Reserve. Cook the salt pork in a dutch oven until crisp. Add onion and cook just until soft but not browned. Add the clam broth from fresh or canned clams and potatoes. Cover and simmer about 20 minutes, or until potatoes are tender. Stir in butter, milk, cream, salt, pepper, and clams. Heat thoroughly, but do not boil. Split crackers and put in a heated tureen. Pour chowder into tureen and serve with additional crackers.

Bean Chowder

4 to 8 servings

1 cup dried pea beans
¾ cup chopped salt pork
1 medium onion, finely chopped
1 cup cubed potatoes

1 cup chopped celery, with leaves
3 sprigs parsley, chopped
2 cups hot milk
Salt and pepper to taste

Wash and pick over beans. Cover with cold water and let soak overnight. Drain. Cover with water in a large kettle. Bring to a boil, lower heat, and simmer 1 to 2 hours, or until beans are tender. Set aside. In a heavy kettle sauté salt pork and onion until lightly browned. Add potatoes, celery, parsley, and beans with liquid. Cover kettle and simmer 30 minutes, or until vegetables are tender. Stir in hot milk and season to taste with salt and pepper.

Corn Chowder   *6 servings*

⅓ cup diced salt pork
1 onion, sliced
3 cups diced potatoes
2¼ cups fresh corn cut from cob

4½ cups hot milk
1½ teaspoons salt
⅛ teaspoon pepper
6 large hard crackers

Fry the salt pork in a heavy chowder kettle. Add onion and cook until soft but not browned. Add potatoes and 3 cups boiling water. Cover and simmer 15 minutes. Add corn, hot milk, and seasonings. Heat, but do not boil. Stir in crackers and serve at once.

Note: *The Pennsylvania Dutch made—and still make—a corn chowder with dried corn, which, though it requires longer cooking, produces soup similar to this one.*

Potato Chowder   *5 to 6 servings*

Potatoes were an ingredient common to many chowders. When there were no meat bones, no fish or shellfish, no game to go into the pot, then potatoes had to be the chief ingredient in a rib-sticking dish.

3 cups diced potatoes
¾ cup chopped celery
½ cup chopped onions
5 cups milk

5 tablespoons butter
1 teaspoon salt
Freshly ground pepper to taste
Chopped parsley

Place potatoes, celery, and onion in a saucepan. Add just enough boiling water to cover. Cook until tender, by which time most of the water should be absorbed. Heat milk, but do not boil. Combine milk with the cooked vegetables. Add butter, salt, and pepper. Heat do not boil. Garnish with parsley.

Parsnip Chowder   *6 to 8 servings*

5 strips bacon
1 large onion, thinly sliced
1½ pounds parsnips, peeled, cored, and
   cut in small cubes
1½ pounds potatoes, peeled and
   cut in small cubes

3 cups milk
3 tablespoons butter
1 cup heavy cream
Salt and freshly ground pepper to taste
Chopped parsley

Cut bacon in small pieces. Cook until crisp and lightly browned. Remove bacon with a slotted spoon and drain on absorbent paper. Cook onion in bacon fat until soft and very lightly browned. Remove onion and place in a heavy dutch oven; reserve bacon fat. Add parsnips, potatoes, and 2 cups boiling water to dutch oven. Cover tightly and cook about 30 minutes, or until vegetables are tender. Add milk and heat, but do not boil. Stir in butter, cream, and reserved bacon fat and season to taste with salt and pepper. Pour hot soup into a heated tureen and sprinkle with bacon bits and chopped parsley. Serve with common crackers or oyster crackers.

II
Breads, Biscuits, and Griddle Cakes

Nothing is more delightful than the smell of fresh hot bread wafting through the house. Bread was usually made at home in colonial days— and is well worth making today. When there was not enough time to let a yeast bread rise, the colonial cook baked with a form of baking soda, or quick-cooked her bread as griddle cakes. Huge wooden dough bowls with sloping sides, often rectangular—perhaps because that was the simplest shape to hollow out of a log—were used for mixing and raising bread dough, because of course bread was not baked one or two loaves at a time. In this section of breads of another day, recipes have been cut to one- and two-loaf yields to suit today's smaller families.

Anadama Bread

2 *loaves*

There are many stories that attempt to explain the unusual name of this delicious bread. One tells of a fisherman in the Massachusetts Bay Colony whose wife, Anna, was apparently not at all an inventive cook—she served him, day after day, cornmeal mush with a little molasses to pour over it. One day, in desperation, the fisherman added flour and yeast to the cornmeal and molasses and baked the resulting mixture. When he sat down to eat his sweet-smelling loaf, he was heard to mutter, "Anna, damn her!" A second story tells of the woman who first baked it, who was apparently something of a gadabout. When her husband came home and found her missing, it was his custom to go through the house muttering, "Where am 'er, damn 'er!"

7 to 8 cups unsifted all-purpose flour, divided	*2 packages active dry yeast*
1¼ cups yellow cornmeal	*⅓ cup butter, softened*
2½ teaspoons salt	*⅔ cup molasses, at room temperature*

In large bowl of electric mixer thoroughly combine 2½ cups flour with the cornmeal, salt, and yeast. Add softened butter and molasses. Gradually add 2½ cups very warm tap water (120–130°) and beat 2 minutes at medium speed of electric mixer, scraping bowl occasionally. Add ½ cup flour. Beat at high speed 2 minutes, scraping bowl occasionally. Stir in enough additional flour to make a stiff dough. Turn out onto a lightly floured board and knead until smooth and elastic, about 8 to 10 minutes. Place in a greased bowl, turning once to grease top. Cover; let rise in a warm place, free from draft, until doubled in bulk, about 1 hour. Meanwhile, grease two 9- x 5- x 3-inch loaf pans. When dough has doubled in bulk, punch it down and divide in half. Shape into loaves and place in loaf pans. Cover; let rise in a warm place, free from draft, until doubled in bulk, about 45 minutes. While loaves are rising, preheat oven to 375°. Bake 45 minutes, or until done. Remove from pans and cool on wire racks.

Cracklin' Bread

6 *servings*

¾ cup finely diced salt pork	*1 teaspoon salt*
2 cups cornmeal	*2 eggs, well beaten*
1½ teaspoons baking powder	*1 cup buttermilk*
½ teaspoon baking soda	

Grease an 11- x 7- x 1½-inch baking pan. Preheat oven to 400°. Fry salt pork in a skillet over low heat until brown and well cooked. Remove browned bits of salt pork, called cracklings, from fat and place on absorbent paper to drain. Reserve fat. Sift together cornmeal, baking powder, baking soda, and salt. Combine eggs, buttermilk, and 2 tablespoons of the reserved salt pork drippings. Stir into cornmeal mixture, together with cracklings. Blend well. Spread in baking pan and bake 25 to 30 minutes. Serve hot.

Cornmeal Yeast Bread

2 loaves

5½ to 6 cups all-purpose flour,
  divided
1 cup yellow cornmeal
2 packages active dry yeast
2 cups milk
¾ cup butter or margarine

½ cup sugar
1½ teaspoons salt
2 eggs
Melted butter
Sesame seeds

In large bowl of electric mixer combine 2 cups flour, cornmeal, and yeast. In a 1-quart saucepan combine milk, butter, sugar, and salt; heat over low heat until warm but not hot (120–130°). Add to flour mixture and stir well. Beat in eggs. Beat ½ minute at low speed of electric mixer, scraping bowl constantly, then beat 3 more minutes at high speed. Add 1 cup flour and beat 1 minute longer. With a wooden spoon, stir in enough remaining flour to make a soft dough. Turn out onto a lightly floured surface; knead 5 to 10 minutes, or until smooth and satiny. Place in a greased bowl, turning once to grease top. Cover bowl. Let rise in a warm place, free from draft, until doubled in bulk, about 1 hour. (If room is drafty, place dough in an un-heated oven with a pan of warm water on rack below bread.) Meanwhile, grease two 9- x 5- x 3-inch loaf pans. Punch dough down; divide in half. On a lightly floured surface roll each half into a 9- x 12-inch rectangle. Beginning with the 9-inch edge, roll dough tightly; seal final seam well with thumbs. Seal ends of loaf and fold under. Place in loaf pans, seam side down. Brush with melted butter; sprinkle tops with sesame seeds. Cover and let rise in a warm place, free from draft, until doubled in bulk, about 1 hour. Preheat oven to 375°. Bake 35 to 40 minutes, or until loaf sounds hollow when tapped. Turn out of pans onto wire rack to cool.

Apple Corn Bread

8 servings

Apples, well remembered from the home country, were the most plentiful fruit in New England. Usually they took their place in desserts and in pre-serves, but occasionally they gave a welcome different flavor to too-familiar foods, as they do in this corn bread.

2 cups white cornmeal
¼ cup sugar, divided
½ teaspoon salt
1 teaspoon cream of tartar
1 teaspoon baking soda

1½ cups milk
3 to 4 tart apples, peeled, cored,
  and thinly sliced
1 teaspoon ground cinnamon

Preheat oven to 375°. Grease well an 8- x 11-inch baking pan. In a bowl mix cornmeal, 2 tablespoons sugar, salt, cream of tartar, and baking soda. Add milk and beat until smooth. Turn into baking pan. Cover with overlapping layers of apple. Combine remaining sugar and cinnamon and sprinkle over top of apples. Bake 30 to 35 minutes, or until a toothpick inserted in center of bread comes out clean.

Old-Fashioned Potato Bread

2 loaves

1 medium potato, peeled and diced
2 packages active dry yeast
2 tablespoons butter, softened
2 tablespoons sugar

1 tablespoon salt
1 cup milk
6½ to 7½ cups unsifted all-purpose
   flour, divided

Place potato in boiling water to cover and cook until tender. Drain, reserving liquid. Add enough hot water to potato liquid to make 1 cup; cool to warm (105–115°). Mash potato and set aside. Pour warm potato water into a large warm bowl. Sprinkle in yeast; stir until dissolved. Add butter, sugar, and salt. Heat milk over moderate heat until warm but not hot (105–115°). Add to potato water mixture along with mashed potato and 3 cups of the flour. Beat until smooth. Stir in enough additional flour to make a stiff dough. Turn out onto a lightly floured board; knead until smooth and elastic, about 8 to 10 minutes. Place in a greased bowl, turning once to grease top. Cover; let rise in a warm place, free from draft, until doubled in bulk, about 35 minutes. Punch dough down; turn over in bowl. Cover and let rise again, about 20 minutes. Meanwhile, grease two 9- x 5- x 3-inch loaf pans. Punch dough down. Turn out onto a lightly floured board and divide in half. Shape each half into a loaf. Place in loaf pans. Cover; let rise in warm place, free from draft, until doubled in bulk, about 50 minutes. Preheat oven to 375°. Dust with flour. Bake 40 minutes. Cool on racks.

Rye Bread

2 loaves

5 cups unsifted all-purpose flour
4 cups unsifted rye flour
2 cups milk
1 tablespoon salt
⅓ cup dark molasses

¼ cup butter
1¼ cups warm ale (105–115°)
2 packages active dry yeast
½ teaspoon fennel seed (optional)

Combine flours and set aside. Scald milk; stir in salt, molasses, and butter. Cool to lukewarm. Measure ale into a large warm bowl. Sprinkle in yeast; stir until dissolved. Stir in lukewarm milk mixture, fennel seed, and 4 cups of the flour mixture. Beat until smooth. Let batter rise in a warm place, free from draft, until doubled in bulk, about 30 minutes. Stir batter down; stir in enough additional flour mixture to make a stiff dough. (Use additional all-purpose flour if needed.) Turn out onto a lightly floured board; knead until smooth and elastic, about 12 minutes. Place in a greased bowl, turning once to grease top. Cover and let rise in a warm place, free from draft, until doubled in bulk, about 45 minutes. Grease two baking sheets. Punch dough down and divide in half. Form each half into a smooth, round ball. Flatten each ball into a mound about 7 inches in diameter. Place on baking sheets. Cover; let rise in a warm place, free from draft, until doubled in bulk, about 50 minutes. Preheat oven to 375°. Bake about 35 minutes, or until browned and done. Remove from baking sheet and cool on wire racks.

Raisin Rye Bread

2 loaves

2¾ to 3½ cups all-purpose flour,
  divided
2 packages active dry yeast
2 cups milk
¼ cup light molasses
2 tablespoons butter

1 tablespoon sugar
2 teaspoons salt
1 cup seedless raisins
1 teaspoon grated lemon peel
2 cups bohemian-style rye and whole-
  wheat flour

In large bowl of electric mixer combine 2 cups all-purpose flour and yeast.
In a 1-quart saucepan combine milk, molasses, butter, sugar, and salt. Heat
over low heat until warm but not hot (120–130°). Add to flour. Beat ½ minute at low speed of electric mixer, scraping bowl constantly, then beat 3 more
minutes at high speed. Add 1 cup all-purpose flour and beat 1 minute longer. Add raisins and lemon peel. Stir in rye and whole-wheat flour and
enough remaining all-purpose flour to make a soft dough. Turn out onto a
lightly floured surface and knead 5 to 10 minutes, or until smooth and
satiny. Place in a greased bowl, turning once to grease top. Cover bowl;
let rise in a warm place, free from draft, until doubled in bulk, about 1
hour. (If room is drafty, place in an unheated oven with a large pan of
warm water on the rack below the bread.) Grease a baking sheet. Punch
dough down and divide in half. Shape each half into a round loaf; flatten
slightly. Place on baking sheet. Cover and let rise in a warm place, free from
draft, until doubled in bulk, about 1 hour. Preheat oven to 375°. Bake
25 to 30 minutes, or until loaf sounds hollow when tapped. Remove to
wire rack to cool.

Sally Lunn

1 large loaf

1 package active dry yeast
1 cup warm milk
½ cup butter, softened
¼ cup sugar

2 teaspoons salt
3 eggs, well beaten
5½ to 6 cups unsifted all-purpose
  flour, divided

Measure ½ cup warm water (105–115°) into a large warm bowl. Sprinkle
in yeast and stir until dissolved. Add milk, butter, sugar, salt, and eggs.
Stir in 3 cups flour. Beat until well blended, about 1 minute. Stir in enough
remaining flour to make a soft dough. Cover and let rise in a warm place,
free from draft, until doubled in bulk, about 1 hour. Grease a 10-inch tube
pan well and dust with flour. Stir down the dough; spoon into pan. Cover;
let rise in a warm place, free from draft, until doubled in bulk, about 1
hour. Preheat oven to 400°. Bake about 30 minutes, or until done. Remove
from pan and cool on wire rack.

Note: *Rather thickly sliced, leftover Sally Lunn makes delicious toast—crisp on
the outside, soft within.*

Bohemian Bread

2 loaves

5 to 5½ cups bohemian-style rye and
   wheat flour, divided
2 packages active dry yeast
2 cups milk

¼ cup butter
3 tablespoons sugar
4 teaspoons salt
⅓ cup dark molasses

In large bowl of electric mixer combine 2 cups flour and yeast. In a 1-quart saucepan combine milk, butter, sugar, and salt. Heat over low heat until warm but not hot (120–130°). Stir in molasses. Add to flour mixture. Beat ½ minute at low speed of electric mixer, scraping bowl constantly, then beat 3 more minutes at high speed. Add 1 cup flour and beat 1 minute longer. Stir in enough remaining flour to make a soft dough. Turn out onto lightly floured surface and knead 5 to 10 minutes, or until smooth and satiny. Place in a greased bowl, turning once to grease top. Cover bowl. Let rise in a warm place, free from draft, until doubled in bulk, about 1 hour. (Or set bread in an unheated oven with a large pan of warm water on rack below bread.) Meanwhile, grease two 9- x 5- x 3-inch loaf pans. Punch dough down and divide in half. On the lightly floured surface roll each half into a 9- x 12-inch rectangle. Beginning with the 9-inch edge, roll dough tightly; seal final seam well with thumbs. Seal ends of loaf and fold under. Place in loaf pans, seam side down. Cover and let rise in a warm place, free from draft, until doubled in bulk, about 1 hour. Preheat oven to 375°. Bake 30 to 35 minutes, or until loaf sounds hollow when tapped. Turn out of pans onto rack to cool.

Spider Corn Bread

6 servings

A spider was an iron skillet with a long handle to protect the cook from the heat of the fireplace and with long legs so that the pan could stand above the fire.

1⅓ cups white cornmeal
⅓ cup sifted all-purpose flour
1 teaspoon baking soda
½ teaspoon salt
¼ cup sugar

1 cup buttermilk
2 eggs, well beaten
2 cups milk, divided
2 tablespoons butter

Preheat oven to 350°. Place cornmeal, flour, baking soda, salt, and sugar in a mixing bowl and mix. Add buttermilk, eggs, and 1 cup milk. Beat with a spoon until smooth. Melt the butter in a heavy 9-inch skillet, and when pan is very hot pour in batter. Slowly and carefully pour last cup of milk over top of batter. Bake about 50 minutes or until cornbread is lightly browned on the top. Cut in wedges and serve at once.

Whole-Wheat Bran Bread

2 loaves

¾ cup milk
1 cup whole-bran cereal
3 tablespoons sugar
4 teaspoons salt
6 tablespoons butter

⅓ cup dark molasses
2 packages active dry yeast
3 cups unsifted whole-wheat flour
2½ to 3 cups unsifted all-purpose flour

Combine milk and 1 cup water in a saucepan; bring to a boil. Stir in cereal, sugar, salt, butter, and molasses. Cool to lukewarm. Measure ½ cup warm water (105–115°) into a large warm bowl. Sprinkle in yeast; stir until dissolved. Add lukewarm cereal mixture and whole-wheat flour; beat until smooth. Add enough all-purpose flour to make a stiff dough. Turn out onto a lightly floured board and knead until smooth and elastic, about 8 to 10 minutes (dough will be slightly sticky). Place in a greased bowl, turning once to grease top. Cover; let rise in a warm place, free from draft, until doubled in bulk, about 1 hour. Grease two 8½- x 4½- x 2½-inch loaf pans. Punch dough down. Turn out onto a lightly floured board; divide in half. Shape into loaves and place in pans. Cover; let rise in a warm place, free from draft, until doubled in bulk, about 1 hour. Preheat oven to 400°. Bake about 30 minutes, or until done. Remove from pans and cool on racks.

Raisin Bread

2 loaves

1 cup warm potato water (105–115°)
2 packages active dry yeast
¾ cup warm milk
¼ cup sugar, divided
¼ cup lukewarm mashed potatoes
6 to 7 cups unsifted all-purpose flour, divided

2 teaspoons salt
2 eggs, beaten
¼ cup butter, melted and cooled
2 cups dark seedless raisins

Measure potato water into a large warm mixing bowl. Sprinkle in yeast and stir until dissolved. Add milk, 2 tablespoons sugar, potatoes, and 2 cups flour. Beat until smooth. Cover and let rise about ½ hour, or until bubbly. Stir down. Add remaining sugar, salt, and 1 cup flour and beat until smooth. Stir in eggs and butter. Add enough additional flour to make a stiff dough. Turn out onto a lightly floured board; knead until smooth and elastic, about 8 to 10 minutes. Place in a greased bowl, turning once to grease top. Cover and let rise in a warm place, free from draft, until doubled in bulk, about 40 minutes. Punch dough down. Turn out onto a lightly floured board and knead in raisins. Divide dough in half. Cover; let rest 5 minutes. Grease two 9- x 5- x 3-inch loaf pans. Roll each dough half into a 9- x 14-inch rectangle. Shape into loaves and place in pans. Cover; let rise in a warm place, free from draft, until doubled in bulk, about 50 minutes. Preheat oven to 350°. Bake bread about 45 minutes, or until browned and done. Remove from pans and cool on wire racks before slicing.

Corn Pone

about 2 dozen servings

½ cup lard
4 cups cornmeal
1½ teaspoons salt

½ teaspoon baking soda
1 cup buttermilk

Grease a baking sheet. Preheat oven to 350°. In a bowl work lard into cornmeal with fingers or a fork. Dissolve salt and baking soda in 1½ cups boiling water. Gradually stir the boiling water into cornmeal mixture. Add just enough buttermilk to make a stiff dough. Shape into a flat circle. Place on baking sheet and bake about 35 minutes, or until done and lightly browned. Cut into triangles.

Note: *Cornmeal was ground at home until industrious millers arrived in the colonies and set up business at sites where water was available to power the big millwheels. Water-ground cornmeal is usually made of whole corn that has not been kiln-dried; it is milled between stones so that heating of the grain or the meal is avoided. It is excellent for simple forms of corn bread and retains the full flavor of the grain, but because of its higher fat content does not keep well, particularly in warm weather. The cornmeal most common today is made of kiln-dried corn ground between rollers; this method produces a high degree of heat, and the product is lower in fat than the water-ground variety. Both white and yellow cornmeal are now used in the North, but white cornmeal is still preferred in the South. When you buy water-ground cornmeal today—usually in health-food stores—be sure that it is refrigerated. Store it in the refrigerator at home, as well.*

Virginia Batter Bread

4 to 6 servings

2 tablespoons butter
1 cup white cornmeal
1½ teaspoons baking soda
1 teaspoon salt

1 tablespoon all-purpose flour
1 egg, well beaten
1 cup buttermilk
1 cup sweet milk

Preheat oven to 450°. Place butter in an 8-inch square pan and heat in hot oven. Combine cornmeal, baking soda, salt, and flour. Mix egg and buttermilk and stir into cornmeal mixture. Add sweet milk and mix batter well. Pour into hot buttered pan. Bake 25 to 30 minutes, or until top tests done. If top is not brown enough, run under a hot broiler for 2 to 3 minutes to brown lightly.

Note: *In the early settler's kitchen there was no convenient broiler under which to place the bread to brown the top. However, a little later, many more elegant establishments boasted a salamander—a flat iron utensil with a long handle—that could be heated in the fire, then passed over the top of any baked food on which a well-browned crust was desired.*

Boston Brown Bread

1 loaf

½ cup rye flour or sifted
  all-purpose flour
1 cup whole-wheat flour
½ cup white cornmeal
½ teaspoon baking powder
½ teaspoon salt

1 teaspoon baking soda
1½ cups buttermilk
½ cup light molasses
1 egg, well beaten
½ cup seedless raisins (optional)

Grease thoroughly a 1-quart mold and its cover. Sift together the flours, cornmeal, baking powder, and salt. Dissolve the baking soda in 1 tablespoon hot water. Combine water mixture, buttermilk, and molasses and blend well. Add the sifted dry ingredients to buttermilk mixture and stir thoroughly until batter is smooth. Add the egg, and the raisins, if desired. Pour batter into the mold and cover tightly. Place on a rack in a large kettle. Add about 2 quarts boiling water. Cover the kettle tightly and simmer about 4 hours, replacing the boiling water as it evaporates. Preheat oven to 400°. When mold is cool enough to handle, lift it from the water. Let stand a few minutes, then turn bread out of mold onto a shallow pan. Bake about 10 minutes, or just long enough to dry it out a little. Slice and serve warm. To reheat, steam in a colander over boiling water 5 to 10 minutes.

Spoon Bread

4 servings

5 tablespoons butter
1 cup water-ground cornmeal
1 teaspoon salt

1 cup cold milk
4 eggs, well beaten

Preheat oven to 425°. Put butter in a 1½-quart baking dish. Place in oven to melt while preparing batter. Combine cornmeal and salt in a mixing bowl. Pour in 2 cups boiling water and stir until smooth. Let stand until mixture cools slightly. Stir in milk. Add eggs and beat with a rotary beater until thoroughly blended. Stir in melted butter. Pour batter into hot baking dish. Bake about 25 minutes, or until set. Serve immediately with extra melted butter.

Potato Scones

4 servings

1 pound potatoes, cooked and mashed
2 tablespoons butter, melted

1 cup sifted all-purpose flour
½ teaspoon salt

Mix all ingredients to make a soft dough. Pat out into a circle about ½-inch thick. Cut in 8 pie-shaped wedges. Heat a griddle over medium heat. Butter hot griddle lightly and cook scones about 4 minutes on each side, or until lightly browned and crisp. Split and serve hot with butter.

Raised Cornmeal Rolls

2½ to 3 dozen

6½ to 7½ cups unsifted all-purpose
flour, divided
1½ cups yellow cornmeal
½ cup sugar
1 tablespoon salt

2 packages active dry yeast
1½ cups milk
½ cup butter
2 eggs, at room temperature

In large bowl of electric mixer thoroughly mix 1½ cups flour, cornmeal, sugar, salt, and dry yeast. Combine milk, ¾ cup water, and butter in a saucepan. Heat over low heat until warm but not hot (120–130°); the butter does not have to melt. Gradually add liquid to dry ingredients and beat 2 minutes at medium speed of electric mixer, scraping bowl occasionally. Add eggs and ½ cup flour. Beat at high speed 2 minutes, scraping bowl occasionally. Stir in enough additional flour to make a stiff dough. Turn out onto a lightly floured board; knead until smooth and elastic, about 8 to 10 minutes. Place in a greased bowl, turning once to grease top. Cover; let rise in a warm place, free from draft, until doubled in bulk, about 1 hour. Meanwhile, grease three 8-inch square baking pans well. Punch dough down and divide into 3 equal pieces. Divide each piece of dough into 9 equal pieces. Form each piece into a smooth ball; place 9 balls in each of the three greased pans. Brush rolls with melted butter. Cover; let rise in a warm place, free from draft, until doubled in bulk, about 1 hour. Preheat oven to 375°. Bake 25 minutes. Remove from pans; cool on wire racks.

Pan Rolls

2 dozen

4½ to 5 cups all-purpose flour, divided
2 packages active dry yeast
1½ cups milk
¼ cup butter

¼ cup sugar
1 teaspoon salt
2 eggs, slightly beaten
Butter

In large bowl of electric mixer combine 1 cup flour and yeast. In a 1-quart saucepan combine milk, butter, sugar, and salt. Heat until warm but not hot (120–130°). Add to flour mixture. Add eggs. Beat ½ minute at low speed of electric mixer, scraping bowl constantly, then 3 more minutes at high speed. Add 1 cup flour and beat 1 minute longer. Stir in enough remaining flour to make a soft dough. Turn out onto a lightly floured surface; knead 5 to 10 minutes, or until smooth and satiny. Place in a greased bowl, turning once to grease top. Cover bowl; let rise in a warm place, free from draft, until doubled in bulk, about 1 hour. (If room is drafty, place bowl in an unheated oven with a large pan of warm water on the rack below the bowl.) Meanwhile, grease a 15- x 10½- x 1-inch jelly roll pan. Punch dough down. Divide into 3 equal parts. Form each part into a long 9-inch roll; cut into 8 equal pieces. Form each piece into a smooth ball and place in pan. Cover and let rise in a warm place, free from draft, until doubled in bulk, 30 to 40 minutes. Preheat oven to 375°. Bake 20 minutes. Serve hot with butter.

Corn Dodgers

1 dozen

1½ cups white cornmeal
1 teaspoon salt

½ cup butter

Preheat oven to 450°. Put the cornmeal and salt in a bowl. Combine butter and 1¼ cups water in a saucepan and bring to a boil. Remove from heat and stir into cornmeal to make a thick mush. Drop by spoonfuls onto baking sheet. Bake about 20 minutes, or until lightly brown on top. Serve at once with butter and jam or honey.

Note: The earliest and simplest cornmeal breads baked by the settlers were combinations of only cornmeal, salt, and water. They were called ash cakes, because they were made in the following manner: Pieces of dough of convenient size were laid on the hearth in front of the fire until their tops had dried out a bit; then ashes were drawn over the cakes, which continued to cook until they were done. When the ashes were brushed off, the cakes were ready to eat. A refinement was to cover the tops of the cakes with green leaves before putting on the ashes—this kept the tops of the cakes cleaner. Travelers simply threw pieces of the dough into the ashes of their campfires to cook.

Cinnamon Rolls

1 dozen

2 to 2¼ cups all-purpose flour, divided
1 package active dry yeast
¾ cup milk
¼ cup butter
Sugar

¾ teaspoon salt
1 egg
Melted butter
1 teaspoon cinnamon
¼ cup seedless raisins (optional)

In large bowl of electric mixer combine 1 cup flour and yeast. In a 1-quart saucepan combine milk, butter, ¼ cup sugar, and salt. Heat over low heat until warm but not hot (120–130°). Add to flour. Add egg. Beat ½ minute at low speed of electric mixer, scraping bowl constantly, then beat 3 more minutes at high speed. Add ½ cup flour and beat 1 minute longer. Stir in enough remaining flour to make a soft dough. Turn out onto a lightly floured surface; knead 5 to 10 minutes, or until smooth and satiny. Place in a greased bowl, turning once to grease top. Cover bowl. Let rise in a warm place, free from draft, until doubled in bulk, about 1 hour. (Or place in an unheated oven with a large pan of warm water on the rack below the dough.) Meanwhile, grease a 9-inch square pan. Punch dough down. On a lightly floured surface roll dough out to a rectangle 8 x 15 inches. Brush with melted butter to within ½ inch of edge. Combine 3 tablespoons sugar with cinnamon and sprinkle over dough. Sprinkle with raisins, if desired. Roll lengthwise as for a jelly roll. Cut into 1¼-inch slices and place in pan, cut side up. Cover and let rise in a warm place, free from draft, until doubled in bulk, about 30 to 40 minutes. Preheat oven to 375°. Bake 25 to 30 minutes, or until lightly browned. Remove to wire rack to cool. Brush with melted butter and sprinkle with sugar.

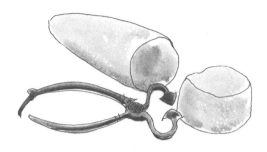

Dough Nuts.

To one pound of flour, put one quarter of a pound of butter, one quarter of a pound of sugar, and two spoonfuls of yeast; mix them all together in warm milk or water, of the thickness of bread, let it raise, and make them in what form you please, boil your fat (consisting of hog's lard), and put them in.

Doughnuts *about 4 dozen*

4 cups sifted all-purpose flour
½ teaspoon salt
½ cup sugar
1 package active dry yeast

1 cup milk
½ cup butter
Fat or oil for deep-frying

In a mixing bowl combine the flour, salt, sugar, and yeast. Heat milk until bubbles appear around the edges. Add butter to hot milk and stir until butter is melted. Let mixture cool to lukewarm. Add flour mixture and stir thoroughly to make a stiff batter. Cover bowl with plastic wrap or aluminum foil and let stand in a warm place until double in bulk. In a deep-fat fryer or deep kettle heat lard, shortening, or cooking oil to 375°. Stir batter down. Scoop up pieces of dough with a teaspoon and drop into hot fat. As doughnuts rise to the surface, turn and continue cooking until brown and cooked. Remove from hot fat with a slotted spoon and drain on absorbent paper. Dust with confectioners sugar, if desired.

Note: *Make the doughnuts very small—otherwise the centers will not cook and the doughnuts will be raw and unpleasant. This dough is stiff enough so that it can be rolled out and cut into large doughnuts, with holes, if desired.*

Pennsylvania Dutch Strickle Sheets   *4 dozen*

4 to 5 cups unsifted all-purpose flour,
  divided
1¼ cups sugar, divided
¾ teaspoon salt

2 packages active dry yeast
1 cup milk
6 tablespoons butter, divided
2 eggs, at room temperature

In large bowl of electric mixer thoroughly mix 1½ cups flour, ½ cup sugar, salt, and yeast. Combine milk, ¼ cup water, and 3 tablespoons butter in a saucepan. Set remaining butter aside to soften. Heat liquid mixture over low heat until warm but not hot (120–130°); the butter does not have to melt. Gradually add to dry ingredients and beat 2 minutes at medium speed of electric mixer, scraping bowl occasionally. Add eggs and 1 cup flour. Beat at high speed 2 minutes, scraping bowl occasionally. Stir in enough additional flour to make a soft dough. Turn out onto a lightly floured board; knead until smooth and elastic, about 8 to 10 minutes. Place in a greased bowl, turning once to grease top. Cover; let rise in a warm place, free from draft, until doubled in bulk, about 45 minutes. Meanwhile, grease three 8-inch square baking pans. Punch dough down. Turn out onto a lightly floured board; divide into 3 equal parts. Roll each part into an 8-inch square, then cut each square into 16 squares. Place squares side by side in the three greased pans. Combine remaining sugar, softened butter, and 2 tablespoons flour. Mix thoroughly. Stir in 2 tablespoons hot water and beat until smooth. Spread over top of squares in pans. Cover and let rise in a warm place, free from draft, until doubled in bulk, about 1 hour. Preheat oven to 400°. Bake 25 to 30 minutes, or until lightly browned and done. Remove from pans and cool on wire racks.

Sour Milk Biscuits   *about 3 dozen*

Because there was no refrigeration, sour milk was a common ingredient available to colonial cooks. To make sour milk, add 1 tablespoon of vinegar or lemon juice to each cup of sweet milk; let the mixture stand at room temperature about 15 minutes before using.

4 cups sifted all-purpose flour
1 teaspoon salt
2 teaspoons cream of tartar
2 teaspoons baking soda

2 tablespoons lard
1⅓ to 1½ cups sour milk
Melted butter

Preheat oven to 400°. Grease a baking sheet. Sift together dry ingredients into a bowl. Add lard and rub into flour mixture with fingertips. Stir in just enough sour milk to make a stiff dough. Roll out to ½-inch thickness on a lightly floured board. Cut into 2-inch rounds. Place close together on baking sheet. Brush tops with melted butter. Bake 15 to 20 minutes, or until golden brown on top.

Minute Biscuits

about 3 dozen

4 cups sifted all-purpose flour
½ teaspoon baking soda
1 teaspoon cream of tartar

¼ cup butter or shortening
1 cup milk

Grease a baking sheet. Preheat oven to 425°. Sift flour, baking soda, and cream of tartar together. Cut in butter with two knives, or work it in with the fingertips. Add milk and stir to make a smooth dough. Pat out to ½-inch thickness on a floured board and cut into 2-inch rounds. Place rounds close together on baking sheet. Bake 12 to 15 minutes, or until lightly browned. Serve piping hot.

Beaten Biscuits

about 2 dozen

2 cups all-purpose flour
½ teaspoon salt

1 teaspoon sugar
2 tablespoons lard

Sift together flour, salt, and sugar. Cut in lard with two knives until mixture is blended. Stir in ⅛ to ½ cup water, enough to make a stiff dough. Knead together thoroughly. Place dough on a flat surface and beat with a heavy mallet, the flat side of an axe, or some other heavy object for 30 minutes, or until dough is elastic. The dough also may be kneaded with the hands until it pops with every pressure of the hand, which will take about 30 minutes. Preheat oven to 325°. Form pieces of dough into small balls, about the size of walnuts. Flatten each with a rolling pin and prick the center with a fork. Place on a baking sheet and bake 30 to 35 minutes, or until lightly browned.

Note: *In the southern homes where these biscuits were most popular there were usually several pairs of sturdy arms and hands to share the task of beating them. Split and buttered, sandwiched with thin slivers of Smithfield ham, Beaten Biscuits graced many a cold collation in Virginia and the Carolinas.*

Honey Nut Bread

1 loaf

2½ cups sifted all-purpose flour
½ teaspoon salt
1 teaspoon baking soda
2 tablespoons butter
1 cup honey

1 large egg
¾ cup sour milk
¼ cup minced candied orange peel
¾ cup seedless raisins
¾ cup chopped walnuts

Grease a 10- x 5- x 3-inch loaf pan. Preheat oven to 300°. Sift together dry ingredients. Cream butter and honey together until light and fluffy. Beat in egg. Add flour mixture alternately with sour milk, beginning and ending with the flour mixture. Add peel, raisins, and nuts and stir until smooth. Pour into loaf pan. Bake about 1 hour 45 minutes, or until a toothpick inserted in center of loaf comes out clean.

Blueberry Gingerbread

6 to 8 servings

1½ cups fresh blueberries
½ cup butter
½ cup sugar
2 eggs, lightly beaten
1 cup buttermilk

1 cup molasses
2½ cups all-purpose flour
1 teaspoon baking soda
1 tablespoon ground ginger

Grease and flour a 9-inch ring mold. Preheat oven to 350°. Rinse blueberries in a colander and spread on absorbent paper to dry thoroughly. Cream butter and sugar together until fluffy. Add eggs, buttermilk, and molasses and mix thoroughly. Sift together flour, baking soda, and ginger. Add flour mixture to molasses mixture, stirring until well blended. Do not overbeat. Carefully fold in blueberries. Pour into ring mold. Bake about 40 minutes, or until a cake tester inserted in cake comes out clean. Unmold onto a serving plate while warm.

Massachusetts Johnnycakes

about 10 cakes

½ cup white cornmeal
½ teaspoon salt
3 tablespoons molasses

1 cup suet, finely chopped
Milk

Combine cornmeal and salt in a bowl. Add about ½ cup of boiling water until every grain of cornmeal swells and the mixture becomes a crumbly mass. Add molasses and suet. Stir in just enough milk to make a batter that will hold its shape when spoonfuls are dropped on the griddle. Drop onto a hot greased griddle and cook slowly until well browned on both sides.

Rhode Island Jonnycakes

about 16 cakes

The reason for the name of these cakes has been obscured. One likely idea is that "jonny" is a corruption of "journey," and that these were originally Journey Cakes, baked and carried along by travelers to provide food for the trip. The battle over the correct spelling of the name—with or without the "h"—is still going on today.

1 cup white cornmeal
1 teaspoon salt

½ cup (about) milk

Combine cornmeal and salt in a bowl. Gradually stir in 1 cup boiling water until every grain of cornmeal swells and the mixture becomes a crumbly mass. When cornmeal is all wet and swollen, add milk gradually, until batter is just a little thicker than regular pancake batter. Heat and lightly grease a heavy griddle. Drop by spoonfuls on griddle and cook thoroughly on one side before turning to cook the other side. It will take a little longer to cook these cakes than regular pancakes. Serve hot with butter and maple syrup.

Buck-Wheat Cakes.

Take milk-warm water, a little salt, a table spoonful of yeast, and then stir in your buck-wheat till it becomes of the thickness of batter; and then let it enjoy a moderate warmth for one night to raise it, bake the same on a griddle, greasing it first to prevent them from sticking.

Buckwheat Cakes   *6 servings*

1 package active dry yeast   *2 cups milk*
¼ teaspoon salt   *3 cups buckwheat flour*

Combine yeast and ¼ cup warm water in a large mixing bowl. Let stand 5 minutes. Stir in salt. Heat milk until bubbles appear around edge. Cool to lukewarm. Stir into yeast. Stir in buckwheat and beat until smooth. Cover bowl with plastic wrap or aluminum foil and let stand in a warm place overnight. In the morning preheat and grease a griddle. Stir the batter down, then drop by spoonfuls onto griddle. Cook until lightly browned on both sides. Serve with butter and maple syrup.

Note: *This mixture is very bland; for additional flavor you may want to add ¼ cup molasses. In the morning, if the batter is too stiff, stir in a little warm milk before frying the cakes.*

Blueberry–Rice Griddle Cakes   *1 dozen*

2 cups fresh blueberries
¼ cup sugar
2 cups dairy sour cream
2 teaspoons baking soda
2 eggs, well beaten

1 cup sifted all-purpose flour
1 cup cooked rice
1 teaspoon salt
2 tablespoons melted butter

Rinse blueberries in a colander and spread on absorbent paper to dry thoroughly. Place in a bowl, sprinkle with sugar, and set aside. Combine sour cream and baking soda and stir into eggs. Stir in flour, rice, salt, and melted butter. Fold in blueberries. Bake on both sides on a hot griddle. This makes thick griddle cakes.

Thick Johnnycakes   *1 dozen*

2 cups stone-ground white cornmeal
1 scant teaspoon salt

Milk
Bacon fat

Preheat oven to 450°. Put cornmeal in an ovenproof bowl and place in oven to heat through, but not long enough to scorch. Remove bowl from oven; stir in salt. Moisten gradually with boiling water, using about 3½ cups in all, or enough to make a very stiff paste. Add sufficient milk just to smooth the dough, about ½ cup. The mixture should be smooth and free of lumps, but not liquid. Heat a heavy griddle or frying pan. Place bacon fat on griddle and heat thoroughly. Drop mixture onto heated griddle in cakes at least ½-inch thick. Cook over low heat about 15 minutes. Lightly press with a pancake turner to smooth out top. Turn and brown 15 minutes on second side. Place on a large baking sheet in a single layer and put in the heated oven just long enough to puff them up a bit. Serve with butter and maple syrup.

Hasty Pudding   *6 to 8 servings*

Bring 2½ cups water and ¾ teaspoon salt to a boil in a deep heavy kettle. When the water is boiling briskly, sprinkle in 1 cup cornmeal, stirring constantly. Reduce heat; simmer over low heat 30 minutes, stirring occasionally. The mixture may be cooked in a double boiler over hot water, in which case it should cook for 1 hour. Serve in deep bowls with plenty of milk, and sweeten to taste with maple syrup, honey, molasses, or sugar.

Fried Hasty Pudding

Rinse an 8- x 5- x 3-inch loaf pan in cold water and fill with cooked Hasty Pudding. Chill well until pudding is firm. Turn pudding out of pan and cut into slices ¾ inch thick. Heat fat in a heavy skillet and pan-fry slices until brown and crusty on both sides. Serve with maple syrup and crisp slices of bacon or browned salt pork.

III
Meat, Fowl,
and Game

Early Americans were hard workers and hearty eaters, and here is a sampling of the satisfying main dishes they enjoyed. From the New England Boiled Dinner to Charleston Chicken Pilau, all are authentic colonial recipes, adapted for modern use—and all are delicious. Some of these dishes—Chicken Smothered in Oysters, for example—sound surprisingly exotic to us. But we must remember that while we use broiler-fryers for the recipe today, the colonial chicken had a long and proud career of egg-laying behind her before she was consigned to the cooking pot, and that oysters were to be had for the gathering all along the coast.

Yankee Pot Roast

Colonial Americans were not blessed with the tender cuts of beef we have today. Pot roast and stew, with their long, slow cooking, were favorite ways of turning the tougher cuts of meat into palatable meals.

1 4- to 5-pound boneless chuck or rump
   roast
Salt and pepper to taste
All-purpose flour for dredging
2 ounces salt pork
1 bay leaf
1 sprig parsley

6 seedless raisins
6 carrots, cut in chunks
6 onions, thickly sliced
6 potatoes, peeled and cut in large
   chunks
2 tablespoons all-purpose flour

Sprinkle meat with salt and pepper and rub with flour. Fry salt pork in heavy dutch oven until crisp and brown. Place meat in hot fat in dutch oven and brown well on all sides. When brown, add enough boiling water to cover the bottom of the pot. Add bay leaf, parsley, and raisins. Cover and simmer slowly 2½ hours. Add carrots, onions, and potatoes. Cover and simmer 30 minutes, or until meat and vegetables are tender. Place meat and vegetables on a heated serving platter. Skim as much fat as possible from top of liquid in pan. Mix 2 tablespoons flour with ½ cup cold water to make a smooth paste. Stir into liquid in pan. Cook, stirring constantly, until mixture boils and thickens. Season to taste if necessary. Serve gravy with pot roast and vegetables.

Spiced Beef

1 4- to 5-pound boneless chuck roast
4 onions
1 teaspoon ground cinnamon
1 teaspoon ground allspice
1 teaspoon ground cloves
1 teaspoon salt

1 teaspoon pepper
Cider vinegar
2 tablespoons butter
4 carrots, finely chopped
1 medium-size yellow turnip, finely
   chopped

Place meat in a deep dish. Chop 2 onions very fine; combine with the spices and sprinkle over top of meat. Cover meat with vinegar. Let stand overnight, turning once. Preheat oven to 275°. Remove meat from liquid and place in a covered roasting pan. Add ½ cup of the vinegar mixture and 2 cups water. Slice the 2 remaining onions and place on top of the meat. Cover pan and roast 2½ hours. Melt butter in a skillet. Add carrots and turnips and cook gently until light brown. Spread vegetables over top of meat and roast about 30 more minutes, or until chuck is very tender. Remove meat from roaster. Skim off as much fat as possible from liquid in pan. Serve sliced meat with pan juices and vegetables and mashed or baked potatoes.

To Stew Beefe. (30)

Cutt Your Beefe into little peices; Season it well with Pepper, & salt, putt it into the Pott you stew it in, with as much water as will cover it, & a pinte of good strong Ale, 2. or 3. Onyons, & a Crust of brown bread; then stew it till it is very tender. About an hour before it is enough, skimme off the fatt & ... some sweete Herbs & putt in a little Thyme, sweete Marjoram, & Winter= =Savoury; scrape a couple of Carrotts, & stew them with your meate, till they are tender; then take them out, & lay them by, till your meate is enough, which must be very tender, lay some toasted bread, at the bottome of the dish; pour your meate & Liquour upon them; Chop your Carrotts in little bitts, & strew them over your Meate, & serve it up; This will take about 4 hours stewing.

Beef Stew
4 to 6 servings

2 pounds beef stew meat, cut in cubes
Salt and pepper to taste
1 can or bottle (12 ounces) ale
3 onions, cut in pieces
1 slice, preferably the end crust, rye or pumpernickel bread, broken in pieces

¼ teaspoon thyme
¼ teaspoon marjoram
¼ teaspoon savory
6 carrots, cut in chunks

Place beef in a dutch oven. Add salt and pepper and 1 cup water. Add ale, onion, and bread. Bring to a boil. Lower heat, cover, and simmer about 2 hours, or until beef is almost tender. Add thyme, marjoram, savory, and carrots. Cover and cook about 30 minutes, or until carrots and meat are very tender.

Note: *This is a very tasty beef stew. To reproduce the original flavor, it should be cooked with the very strong ale recommended in the original recipe. If you use a mild ale or beer, omit the herbs, because their flavor will mask the taste of the ale. Try cooking some potatoes in the stew along with the carrots. They are a more traditional accompaniment than toast, and with them the dish will serve more people.*

Meatballs with Cranberry Sauce

4 to 5 servings

1 pound ground beef
½ cup dry bread crumbs
1 egg
2 tablespoons minced onion

2 teaspoons salt
⅛ teaspoon pepper
2 tablespoons butter
1 cup jellied cranberry sauce

Combine beef, bread crumbs, egg, onion, and seasonings. Blend well and form into small balls. Heat a large skillet and melt butter in skillet. Add meatballs and brown well on all sides. Combine cranberry sauce with ½ cup water. Pour over meatballs. Cover and simmer 45 minutes.

Boiled Dinner

6 servings

4 pounds corned beef brisket
6 small beets, cleaned
4 turnips, peeled

6 carrots, cleaned
1 small head cabbage, cut in sixths
8 peeled potatoes

Place beef in a deep kettle and cover with cold water. Bring to a boil and boil 15 minutes; skim off top. Reduce heat and simmer 3 to 4 hours, or until meat is tender. During the last hour of cooking add beets, turnips, carrots, and cabbage. Thirty minutes before meat is done add the potatoes. When ready to serve, slip skins from the beets. Place meat on a large serving platter and surround with vegetables. Cool the cooking liquid, remove fat, and save the stock for hash on the following day.

Original Plymouth Succotash

12 servings

1 quart pea beans
1 4- to 5-pound stewing chicken
1 4-pound corned beef
1 turnip, sliced

6 potatoes, peeled and sliced
Salt to taste
2 quarts corn, cut from the cob and
   cooked

Pick over beans; cover with water and let stand overnight. Cut chicken in serving pieces and place in a large kettle with corned beef. Cover and simmer 2 hours, or until beef is tender. Cool. Drain beans; cover with water and bring to a boil, then simmer 1 to 2 hours, or until tender. When beans are very tender, drain and mash. Skim fat from chicken and beef stock. Reheat chicken and beef in stock. Remove chicken and beef and keep warm. To hot stock add turnip and potatoes and cook 20 to 25 minutes, or until nearly tender. Add mashed bean pulp, salt to taste, and corn. Cook, stirring very often, until thoroughly heated. Serve chicken and meat on a platter and vegetables in a large tureen.

Note: *As you can see from this recipe, succotash was not, in colonial times, the corn-and-beans side dish we know by this name today. It was, rather, a whole meal in itself, and if a piece of corned beef or a chicken was not available, game—bear was a favorite—was used instead.*

Red Flannel Hash

Use all the vegetables and meat left over from the Boiled Dinner. Cook extra potatoes if necessary—there should be twice as many potatoes as beets. Chop the meat and vegetables coarsely in a wooden bowl or on a board with a French knife. Do not put through food chopper. Put 1 tablespoon of meat drippings in a heavy skillet. Turn the chopped meat and vegetables into skillet. Sprinkle with salt and pepper if needed. Moisten with some of the stock left from the boiled dinner. Smooth hash flat. Cover and cook slowly until hash is brown and crusted on the bottom. Fold over like an omelet and serve, or turn out on a serving platter upside down.

Corned Beef Hash

4 to 6 servings

3 cups chopped cooked potatoes
4 cups chopped cooked corned beef

¼ cup butter
Freshly ground pepper to taste

Combine potatoes and corned beef. Melt butter in a heavy skillet. Add ¾ cup boiling water or hot broth left from cooking corned beef. Add potatoes and beef mixture. Season to taste with pepper. Cook over very low heat about 15 minutes, or until a brown crust has formed on lower side of hash. Fold over and place on hot serving dish.

Southern Ham

20 or more servings

1 country-cured ham
1 cup dark molasses

Whole cloves
1 cup pickle juice

Soak ham overnight in cold water to cover. The next morning, drain and remove any hard outside surface. Scrub thoroughly. Put in a large pan, skin side down. Cover with water. Add molasses and simmer slowly 20 to 25 minutes for each pound of ham, or until ham is tender when pierced with a fork. Remove from heat and let cool in liquid. Preheat oven to 350°. Remove ham from liquid and carefully remove all skin. Score ham and dot with whole cloves. Pour pickle juice over top of ham. Bake 1 hour, or until top is browned and crisp. When serving, carve in very thin slices parallel to the bone. This ham is very rich.

Note: *The pickle juice used in this recipe not only gave the ham a delightful sweet-sour taste, but also satisfied the desire of the colonial cook not to waste anything, even the liquid left when the pickles were eaten! Some recipes similar to this one call for the addition of grape juice, instead of or in combination with molasses, to the water in which the ham is boiled.*

Fried Salt Pork

3 slices per serving

Cut salt pork in thin slices. Pour hot water over it, let stand about 2 minutes, and drain. Dip the pork slices in 2 beaten eggs. Roll in dry bread crumbs. Fry in hot fat until crisp on both sides. Serve with fried mush.

Smithfield Ham

about 20 servings

Select a ham of about 14 pounds. (Smaller hams have too much bone in proportion to meat and larger ones have too much fat.) Scrub the ham with a stiff brush and place, skin side down, in a pan large enough so that the ham can be covered with water. Soak overnight. Next day, in the same water, bring to a boil and simmer 20 minutes to the pound. Keep covered with water at all times, and cook with the lid on the pan. At end of estimated time, test shank bones. If loose, remove the ham to a baking pan; if not, cook a little longer until the bones are loose. While ham is still warm, remove skin and any bones that are loose enough to take out without tearing the ham. If very fat, cut some fat off, leaving about ½ inch. Preheat oven to 350°. Combine 1 cup brown sugar, 1 tablespoon ground cloves, and 2 tablespoons prepared mustard. Spread over the ham. Bake until well glazed.

Schnitz un Knepp

6 to 8 servings

This recipe came to Pennsylvania with the "Dutch"—who were actually Germans—who helped to settle William Penn's colony. The dish still appears regularly on Pennsylvania Dutch tables today.

3 pounds smoked ham, with bone	4 teaspoons baking powder
3 cups dried apples	3 tablespoons butter
2 tablespoons brown sugar	1 egg, beaten
2 cups sifted all-purpose flour	½ to ⅔ cup milk
½ teaspoon salt	

Put ham in a large kettle. Cover with cold water. Bring to a boil, reduce heat, cover, and simmer gently for 2 hours. While ham is cooking, put dried apples in a bowl and cover with water. When ham has cooked 2 hours, add drained apples and brown sugar. Cover and simmer 1 hour longer. Sift together flour, salt, and baking powder. Cut in butter with 2 knives, or mix with fingers until it is well distributed. Stir in egg. Add enough milk to make a moist, fairly stiff dough. Drop batter by tablespoonfuls into gently boiling ham-apple mixture. Cover tightly and simmer 12 to 15 minutes, or until dumplings are cooked. Arrange ham, apples, and dumplings on a hot platter. Serve with the broth as a sauce.

Fried Salt Pork with Cream Gravy

3 slices per serving

Cut salt pork in thin slices. Fry in hot pork fat until delicately brown. Put in a deep serving dish. Pour fat from skillet, leaving about 1 tablespoonful in bottom of pan. Pour in 1 cup heavy cream. Heat, but do not boil, stirring up bottom of pan to get bits of browned meat. Pour over salt pork in serving dish. Serve with hot whipped potatoes.

Salt Pork in Batter   *3 slices per serving*

½ pound salt pork
⅓ cup milk
1 egg, well beaten
Pinch of salt

¼ teaspoon cream of tartar
⅛ teaspoon baking soda
5 tablespoons all-purpose flour

Cut salt pork in thin slices and remove the rind. Pour boiling water over slices and let stand 5 minutes. Drain. Beat together remaining ingredients. Dip slices of salt pork in batter and fry in hot pork fat until crisp on both sides.

Scrapple   *6 to 8 servings*

1½ pounds pork shoulder
¼ pound pork liver
1 cup yellow cornmeal
2 teaspoons salt
¼ cup minced onion

¼ teaspoon thyme
1 teaspoon sage
1 teaspoon marjoram
½ teaspoon freshly ground pepper

Combine pork shoulder and liver in a kettle. Add 1 quart water. Cover and cook over moderate heat about 1 hour, or until pork is tender. Drain, reserving broth. Chop meat very fine. Blend cornmeal and salt with 1 cup cold water and 2 cups of the reserved broth. Cook, stirring constantly, until thick. Stir in meat, onion, herbs, and pepper. Cover mixture and cook very slowly, stirring occasionally, about 1 hour. Pour mixture into a 9- x 5- x 3-inch loaf pan. Cool, then chill until very firm. Cut in slices about ½ inch thick. Fry in hot fat until brown and crisp on both sides. Serve with scrambled eggs or fried apple rings.

Hog's Head Cheese   *8 to 10 servings*

The early settlers wasted not in the hope of wanting not. This dish, and the preceding recipe for Scrapple, show the delicious uses to which bits and pieces of what we might think of as "useless" meat were put.

1 pound fresh pork pieces (ears, feet,
    nose) or pig's head
1 pound neck of beef

1 teaspoon salt
1¼ teaspoons poultry seasoning
½ teaspoon pepper

Place pork pieces and beef in a kettle. Add 1 cup water and simmer until meat is very tender and falls from bones. Remove bones and skin from meat and chop meat fine. Stir in seasonings. Add just enough water to make a smooth mixture, not too liquid. Heat mixture thoroughly. Pack into a bread pan; chill thoroughly. Remove fat from top of pan and cut in thin slices for serving.

Jellied Pickled Pigs' Feet

6 servings

6 pigs' feet
1 bay leaf
1 large onion, sliced
6 cloves

½ sweet red pepper
1 teaspoon salt
1 bunch parsley
Vinegar

Scrub and scrape pigs' feet thoroughly. Cook in boiling water until tender. Add remaining ingredients, except vinegar. Cook until vegetables are in shreds and the meat drops from the bones. Remove pigs' feet and remove every bit of bone, saving the meat. Remove and discard the bay leaf, cloves, pepper, and parsley. Skim the fat from the liquid and strain liquid into a kettle. Bring to a boil and cook until reduced to about half; you will need enough liquid to cover the meat halfway. Add enough vinegar to make sufficient liquid to cover meat completely. Put meat in a casserole, add vinegar mixture, and mix thoroughly. Let stand 12 hours. Serve very cold.

Chicken Smothered in Oysters

8 servings

2 broiler-fryer chickens, about 2½ pounds each
¼ cup butter
Salt and pepper to taste

1 cup milk
1 quart oysters
2 cups light cream

Preheat oven to 375°. Cut chicken into quarters. Heat butter in a skillet. Add chicken pieces and brown lightly on all sides. Remove from skillet and place in a casserole with a well-fitting lid. Season with salt and pepper. Pour milk over chicken. Cover and bake 45 minutes. Add oysters and cream. Bake uncovered 15 to 20 minutes, or until chicken is tender and oysters are curled.

Southern Fried Chicken

4 servings

1 can (13 ounces) evaporated milk
All-purpose flour
Salt
½ teaspoon poultry seasoning
¼ teaspoon pepper

1 broiler-fryer chicken, cut in serving pieces
Cooking oil or shortening
1 cup chicken broth

Pour evaporated milk into a shallow dish. Combine ½ cup flour, 2 teaspoons salt, poultry seasoning, and pepper. Dip chicken pieces in milk, then roll in flour mixture; reserve remaining milk for gravy. Heat cooking oil or shortening to a depth of ½ inch in a large skillet. Place chicken, skin side down, in skillet. Cook, uncovered, 15 to 25 minutes on each side, turning only once. Remove chicken and keep hot. Drain off all but 2 tablespoons fat. Stir in 2 tablespoons flour and ½ teaspoon salt. Cook, stirring, 1 minute. Remove from heat and stir in broth and reserved milk. Cook, stirring constantly, until mixture thickens. Serve chicken with gravy and biscuits.

Fried Chicken   *8 servings*

¾ cup all-purpose flour
1½ teaspoons salt
¼ teaspoon pepper

2 broiler-fryer chickens, cut in serving
   pieces
Cooking oil or shortening

Combine flour and seasonings. Roll chicken pieces in seasoned flour. Heat oil or shortening to a depth of ½ inch in skillet. Place chicken, skin side down, in skillet, using large, meatier pieces first. Cook, uncovered, 15 to 25 minutes on each side. Drain well on absorbent paper.

Charleston Chicken Pilau   *6 servings*

1½ cups sliced celery
¾ cup coarsely chopped onions
¾ cup diced green pepper
¼ cup butter
2 cups chicken bouillon
1 can (1 pound) tomatoes

2 teaspoons salt
⅛ teaspoon cayenne
1 bay leaf
1 2½-pound broiler-fryer, cut in
   serving pieces
1½ cups raw rice

Cook celery, onion, and green pepper in hot butter in a dutch oven for about 5 minutes, until tender but not browned. Stir in chicken bouillon, tomatoes, salt, cayenne, and bay leaf. Add chicken. Cover and cook over medium heat until chicken is partially cooked, about 20 minutes. Stir in rice. Cover; cook over low heat about 25 minutes. Remove cover and cook until liquid is absorbed and rice is tender, about 5 minutes more.

Note: *Pilaus are typical of Carolina cookery in colonial times. No doubt the idea for this and similar dishes was brought to Charleston, when that city was a great seaport, by some trader who had been to India. Southern cooks changed many of the ingredients and modified the dish so that it came out fluffy and greaseless, unlike its Indian antecedents. Rice is common to all pilaus; from that point ingredients vary greatly from recipe to recipe, some calling for squab, some for okra and/or tomatoes, some for eggs, some for shrimp.*

Maine Chicken Stew   *8 servings*

2 broiler-fryer chickens, 3½ to 4
   pounds each
6 potatoes, peeled and sliced
3 onions, sliced
2 tablespoons butter

1 cup light cream
Salt and pepper to taste
Minced parsley
6 to 8 common crackers

Cut chicken into serving pieces. In a heavy dutch oven place alternate layers of chicken, potatoes, and onion. Cover with cold water. Bring to a boil, lower heat, cover, and simmer 1 to 1½ hours, or until chicken is tender. Add butter and cream. Season to taste with salt and pepper. Add parsley. Split crackers; add to stew as many as desired. Heat before serving.

New Hampshire Chicken

4 to 6 servings

4 cups dried marrow beans
1 4½- to 5-pound stewing chicken
1 pound lean salt pork
4 small onions, peeled

1 teaspoon dry mustard
1½ teaspoons salt
2 tablespoons light molasses

Wash and pick over beans. Place in a kettle, cover with cold water, and let stand overnight. The next morning, drain off the water. Cover with fresh water, bring to a boil, lower heat, and simmer until beans are tender. Remove a few beans on a spoon and blow on them; if the skins pop, the beans are tender. Do not overcook. Clean and truss the chicken. Cover the salt pork with water in a saucepan; bring to a boil. Drain and cut into 4 pieces; score the rind. Place the trussed chicken in the bottom of a heavy dutch oven or large casserole. Drain beans, reserving liquid. Preheat oven to 300°. Put onions in pot with chicken and cover with the cooked beans. Combine mustard, salt, and molasses with ½ cup hot water. Pour mixture over beans. Tuck the 4 pieces of salt pork into top of beans. Add enough of the reserved bean liquid to cover the entire mixture. Cover tightly and bake 6 to 7 hours. Check mixture several times during cooking and add boiling water as necessary to keep beans from drying out. About 15 minutes before serving time, remove cover so that beans and pork will brown on top. Serve from the casserole so that everyone gets some pieces of chicken with the beans. The chicken will have fallen off the bones, which may be removed easily.

Williamsburg Chicken 'n' Ham Bake

6 to 8 servings

½ cup butter, divided
2 cups dry bread cubes
½ cup chopped onions
⅓ cup unsifted all-purpose flour
1 teaspoon salt

2 cups light cream
1 cup milk
½ teaspoon rubbed sage
2 cups cubed cooked ham
3 cups cubed cooked chicken

Preheat oven to 350°. Melt 3 tablespoons butter in a saucepan; toss in bread cubes. Set aside. In a large saucepan melt remaining butter. Add onion and sauté until tender. Stir in flour and salt and cook 1 minute. Remove from heat and stir in cream and milk. Add sage. Cook over moderate heat, stirring constantly, until mixture comes to a full boil. Remove from heat and stir in ham and chicken. Pour mixture into a 12- x 7½- x 2-inch baking dish. Top with bread cubes. Bake about 25 minutes, or until mixture is bubbling and bread cubes are browned.

To ſtuff and roaſt a Turkey, or Fowl.

One pound of ſoft wheat bread, three ounces of beef ſuet, three eggs, a little ſweet thyme, ſweet marjoram, pepper and ſalt, and ſome add a gill of wine ; fill the bird therewith and ſew it up, hang down to a ſteady ſolid fire, baſting frequently with ſalt and water, and roaſt until a ſteam emits from the breaſt, put one third of a pound of butter into the gravy, duſt flour over the bird and baſte with the gravy ; ſerve up with boiled onions and cramberry-ſauce, mangoes, pickles or celery.

2. Others omit the ſweet herbs, and add parſley done with potatoes.

To stuff and roast a Turkey, or Fowl — *about 8 servings*

1 loaf (1 pound) firm white bread	1½ teaspoons salt
½ cup ground or minced beef suet	¼ cup white wine (optional)
3 eggs, beaten	1 10-pound turkey
1 teaspoon thyme	½ lemon
1 teaspoon marjoram	Cooking oil or melted butter for
¼ teaspoon pepper	basting

Crumble the bread or cut into small cubes. Toss lightly with the suet, eggs, thyme, marjoram, pepper, and salt. Add wine or ¼ cup water to moisten. Preheat oven to 325°. Rinse turkey inside and out with cold water. Drain and pat dry. Rub inside of turkey with cut side of lemon. Lightly salt body cavity. Put part of the stuffing in the neck cavity. Fold back the neck skin and fasten with skewers. Stuff body cavity loosely and close opening with skewers. Fold wing tips under bird. Insert a metal skewer through heavy part of each leg, through leg into body of turkey. Loop a string around end of each skewer and tie the ends around the ends of the drumsticks to the tail. Line a shallow roasting pan with aluminum foil. Place turkey on a rack in the pan. Brush with oil or melted butter. Roast 2½ to 3 hours. During the roasting time, when turkey breast turns brown, cover top of turkey with a tent of aluminum foil. Turkey is cooked when a meat thermometer placed in center of the inside thigh muscle or in the thickest part of the breast registers 185°. Test for doneness also by pressing thickest part of drumstick with fingers; if it feels very soft, turkey is done.

Simmered Turkey

If the wild turkeys were as large as we are led to believe, it follows that they probably were very tough—in which case they may very well have been braised or simmered, making a series of meals from the stewpot. This method of cooking would yield good turkey broth to eat plain, or to use as a stock for heavier soups. The stewed turkey pieces would make a meal, with vegetables, and the leftover pieces would make excellent second-day dishes.

Cut the turkey into pieces and place in a large, heavy kettle with a tight-fitting lid. Add ½ to 1 cup water and ½ teaspoon salt for each pound of turkey. Add 1 or 2 small carrots, cut up, 2 small onions, cut up, 2 to 3 stalks celery, and a few peppercorns. Bring water to a rapid boil. Skim any froth from the surface and reduce the heat to simmering. Cook gently 2 to 3 hours, or until thickest pieces are fork tender.

Note: *The turkey pieces can be served with biscuits, mashed potatoes, or dumplings. Leftover turkey should be chilled and used for turkey salad, either hot or cold, creamed turkey on biscuits, or turkey turnovers. The remaining bits and pieces can be combined with the broth and additional vegetables for a rich chowder.*

Spit-Roasted Turkey

The abundant turkeys of colonial times may very well have been cooked on a spit over the hot coals, as a change from the stewing and steaming that were the usual methods of cooking most foods. Here is a modern-day adaptation that would be nice to try on the outdoor barbecue some fall day, perhaps even for Thanksgiving dinner.

Select a turkey weighing from 10 to 12 pounds, or whatever size your spit will hold easily. Wash the bird, remove the giblets and neck, and pat turkey dry. Simmer the giblets and neck in water to make gravy or stock. Sprinkle the cavity with salt and a little thyme, or whatever herb pleases you. Add a stalk or two of celery and a few slices of onion. Truss the turkey securely, keeping the wings and legs close to the body; skewer the neck skin at the back. Drive the spit from a point a little above the tail, pushing through the turkey to come out at about the top of the wishbone. Turn spit in the hands to see that the turkey balances. Fasten with clamps on the spit. Rub the skin with oil, butter, or margarine. Insert a meat thermometer in the thickest part of the thigh. Connect the spit to the motor and cook over medium-hot coals (or in the oven on the spit) until the meat thermometer registers 175°, or until the leg joint moves easily and the thigh meat feels cooked when it is pressed with the fingers. (Use a double thickness of paper towels when pressing the meat so that you won't burn yourself.) As a general rule, allow about 15 minutes cooking time for each pound of turkey. Baste the bird with melted butter or margarine several times during cooking. A turkey this size should make 8 to 10 hearty servings.

Fricassee of Turkey Wings   *4 servings*

4 turkey wings	*½ teaspoon salt*
All-purpose flour	*⅛ teaspoon pepper*
Fat for browning	*Broth or water*

Sprinkle the turkey wings with flour. Brown in a heavy skillet in a small quantity of hot fat. Lower heat and sprinkle with salt and pepper. Add just enough liquid to cover the bottom of the pan. Cover tightly and simmer until tender, about 1½ hours. Add more liquid if needed during cooking time. If desired, thicken gravy with a little flour. Serve with mashed potatoes or biscuits or rice.

Note: *If you would like a heartier dish, cut-up pieces of potatoes, carrots, onion, or any desired vegetable may be added about ½ hour before the wings are tender. Turkey legs may be cooked by the same method.*

Goose with Sauerkraut Stuffing   *8 servings*

1 large onion, chopped	*1 small carrot, grated*
1 tablespoon butter	*2 teaspoons caraway seeds*
6 cups drained sauerkraut	*½ teaspoon salt*
1 medium apple, peeled, cored, and diced	*¼ teaspoon pepper*
1½ cups grated raw potatoes	*½ cup dry white wine (optional)*
	1 11- to 12-pound goose

In a large skillet sauté onion in butter until tender. Add sauerkraut, apple, potatoes, carrot, seasonings, and wine. Simmer about 5 minutes, stirring constantly. Preheat oven to 350°. Remove large pieces of fat from the cavity of the goose. Fill loosely with the stuffing. Use skewers to close the cavity; tie the wings and drumsticks close to the body with string. Place on a rack in a shallow roasting pan. Roast 3½ to 4 hours, or until brown and tender. If the juices run clear when the drumstick is pierced, the goose is cooked.

Game Birds

Wildfowl were prized not only for the food they supplied but also as a source of down for pillows and bedding, and of quills to be sharpened and used as writing pens.

Wild Duck   *2 servings*

Preheat oven to 450°. Wash a 2- to 2½-pound wild duck well, removing any pin feathers. Pat dry. Place on a rack in a shallow roasting pan. Arrange 2 or 3 slices of bacon on the breast. Roast 15 minutes. Reduce oven temperature to 350° and roast 35 to 40 minutes, or until juices run clear, not pink, when a knife point is inserted into the breast. The bacon should be removed after about 20 minutes of roasting time.

Note: *This duck is cooked to a medium stage; some people prefer it rare and others well done. If too well done, however, wild duck tends to be dry.*

Game Birds à l'Orange   6 servings

6 partridges
Salt and pepper to taste
1 pound salt pork
6 to 8 oranges
3 tablespoons butter

3 green onions, minced
¾ teaspoon dried tarragon
6 tablespoons currant jelly
¼ teaspoon dry mustard
¼ teaspoon salt

Preheat oven to 425°. Tie legs and wings with string, close to body of each bird. Season with salt and pepper. Cut salt pork in thin slices and completely cover breast of each bird. Tie in place with string. Roast in a shallow roasting pan 30 minutes. While birds are cooking, prepare sauce. Wash oranges. With a potato peeler remove very thin strips, without the pith, of the peel from one orange. Shred into fine pieces with scissors, making 3 tablespoons shredded peel. Section 3 or 4 oranges to make 1½ cups drained orange sections. Drain sections and measure juice; ream remaining oranges to make 1¼ cups juice. Reserve. In a large skillet melt butter; add green onion and tarragon and cook 2 to 3 minutes. Add orange juice, orange peel, currant jelly, mustard, and salt. Stir mixture and bring to a boil. Remove birds from oven and place in skillet. Cover and simmer gently 15 to 20 minutes. Remove birds to platter. Add orange sections to sauce. Heat quickly and serve with partridges.

Pheasant, Hunter Style   6 to 8 servings

2 pheasants
¼ cup all-purpose flour
1 teaspoon salt
1 teaspoon paprika
2 tablespoons cooking oil
5 tablespoons butter, divided
¾ cup chopped onions

1½ cups mushrooms, halved
¼ cup slivered green pepper
½ cup dry white wine
1 can (1 pound) Italian-style tomatoes
½ bay leaf
1 sprig rosemary, about ¾ inch long
1 tablespoon cornstarch

Preheat oven to 350°. Cut pheasant in serving pieces. Remove skin from pieces. Combine flour, salt, and paprika. Dust pheasant pieces with mixture. Heat oil with 2 tablespoons of the butter in a skillet. Add pheasant and brown each piece slowly. Meanwhile, melt remaining butter in another skillet. Add onion, mushrooms, and green pepper. Cook slowly just until onion is tender. Add wine, tomatoes, bay leaf, and rosemary. Heat to boiling. Arrange browned pheasant pieces in a baking dish. Pour hot sauce over top. Cover and bake 45 minutes to 1 hour, or until pheasant is tender. Remove pheasant pieces to a heated serving dish. Blend cornstarch with 1 tablespoon water. Stir into sauce. Cook over medium heat, stirring until thickened. Pour over pheasant. Serve with hot boiled potatoes tossed with butter and grated lemon peel.

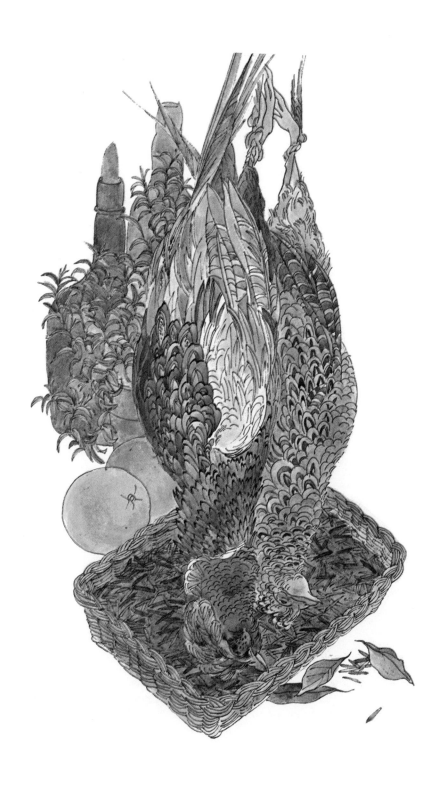

Roast Stuffed Pheasant
5 to 6 servings

One of the many things that the Indians taught the settlers was that stuffing not only adds flavor to meat and fowl, but extends the meat, and is delicious in itself.

1 package (6 ounces) long grain and
   wild rice mix
⅔ cup chopped onions
½ pound mushrooms, sliced
Butter
¼ cup chopped parsley
½ cup toasted blanched slivered
   almonds

Dry sherry
2 young pheasants, about 3 pounds
   each
3 tablespoons all-purpose flour
1 cup milk
1 chicken bouillon cube

Prepare rice mix according to package directions. Preheat oven to 350°. While rice is cooking, sauté onion and mushrooms in ¼ cup hot butter in a large skillet. Remove from heat and stir in parsley, almonds, ¼ cup sherry, and cooked rice. Toss lightly until combined. Fill cleaned pheasants with stuffing; close with skewers or sew with thread. Brush pheasants generously with melted butter, as pheasants tend to be dry. Roast 1¼ to 1½ hours, or until pheasant legs move freely when pressed with fingers. Baste birds often with pan drippings during cooking period. Place pheasants on a warm serving platter and keep warm. Remove 2 tablespoons of the drippings from roasting pan and place in a saucepan. Stir in flour and cook 1 minute. Remove from heat and stir in milk. Cook, stirring constantly, until mixture is smooth and slightly thickened. Dissolve bouillon cube in 2 tablespoons of water. Add to sauce with 2 tablespoons sherry. Simmer about 2 minutes. Serve in a separate dish.

Note: *A game bird popularly known as a pheasant was prevalent throughout the colonies. However, the name pheasant was actually a misnomer, as the bird, also called a heath hen, more closely resembled the grouse or prairie chicken. The heath hen "pheasant" is now extinct, but fortunately we now have an excellent substitute: the European pheasant, which was introduced into North America in the 1800s.*

Potted Pheasant
8 servings

2 pheasants
¼ cup butter
1 teaspoon marjoram

1 teaspoon salt
¼ teaspoon pepper
1 cup dry white wine

Clean pheasants and cut into quarters. Melt butter in a heavy skillet or dutch oven. Brown pheasants in butter, turning often until golden brown on all sides. Add remaining ingredients. Cover tightly and simmer, turning once or twice, for 1 hour, or until very tender. Serve with wild rice and currant jelly.

Ducks à la Mode.

TAKE two fine Ducks, cut them into Quarters, fry them in Butter a little Brown, then pour out all the Fat, and throw a little Flour over them ; add Half a Pint of good Gravy, a Quarter of a Pint of Red Wine, two Shalots, an Anchovy, and a Bundle of Sweet Herbs ; cover them close, and let them stew a Quarter of an Hour ; take out the Herbs, skim off the Fat, and let your Sauce be as thick as Cream. Send it to Table, and garnish with Lemon.

Ducks à la Mode   *4 servings*

1 duckling, cleaned
All-purpose flour for dredging
1 cup chicken bouillon
½ cup dry red wine

2 shallots, coarsely chopped
1 anchovy fillet
Sweet herbs, such as marjoram, thyme,
  rosemary, to taste

Cut duckling into quarters. Brown in a hot skillet or dutch oven. As the duckling browns, pour off accumulated fat. When quarters are well browned, sprinkle with flour. Add bouillon, red wine, shallots, anchovy, and sweet herbs to taste. Cover tightly and simmer about 30 minutes, or until duckling is tender, turning pieces occasionally during cooking time. Remove duckling to a hot platter. Skim off any fat from the top of the gravy. Boil gravy briskly, stirring frequently, until mixture is thick and smooth. Serve with duckling and garnish bird with lemon wedges, if desired.

Note: *It is interesting that in many of the old recipes requiring long, slow cooking, an anchovy was included among the ingredients. In most cases the anchovy was used instead of salt, to give the finished dish some zest. The dish will probably taste better to present-day palates if salt is used rather than an anchovy. You will also find that browning time is rather slow because duckling is much fatter than the wild ducks that were called for in the original recipe.*

Duckling with Apple Stuffing

4 servings

1 4½- to 5-pound duckling
¾ teaspoon salt, divided
1 cup peeled, chopped raw apple
1 cup diced celery
¼ cup chopped onion

⅓ cup melted butter
4 cups ½-inch bread cubes (about 10
  slices bread)
¼ teaspoon leaf thyme

Preheat oven to 325°. Clean, wash, and drain duckling. Pat skin and body cavity gently with paper toweling. Sprinkle ½ teaspoon of the salt evenly in neck and body cavities. Sauté apple, celery, and onion in melted butter until apple is tender. Toss together with bread cubes and thyme, mixing lightly but thoroughly. Fill neck and body cavities loosely with stuffing mixture. Skewer neck skin to back. Cover opening of body cavity with aluminum foil and tie legs together loosely. Place duckling on a rack in a shallow open roasting pan. Bake 2 to 2½ hours, or until duckling is tender and skin is crisp.

Note: *The easiest way to serve duckling is to remove stuffing with a spoon and then cut the duck into quarters with poultry shears.*

Wild Goose

6 to 8 servings

Preheat oven to 350°. Sprinkle a 6- to 8-pound young goose inside and out with the juice of 1 lemon and salt and pepper to taste. Fill body cavity with desired dressing; truss bird. Place breast side up on a rack in a shallow roasting pan. Cover breast with bacon slices and then with cheesecloth soaked in melted bacon fat or cooking oil. Roast 2 to 3 hours, or until tender. If the age of the goose is unknown and you think it may be tough, add 1 cup of water to the pan and cover tightly for the last hour of roasting.

Day-After Pie

4 to 6 servings

3 cups warm cooked rice
¼ cup butter
1 egg, well beaten
Pinch of ground nutmeg

2 to 3 cups leftover cubed venison with
  gravy
Salt and pepper to taste
2 hard-cooked eggs, sliced

Preheat oven to 375°. Mix warm rice with butter, egg, and nutmeg. Butter a 1½-quart casserole well and cover bottom and sides with about two-thirds of the rice mixture. Put cubed meat and gravy in center. If they are already well seasoned, season with very little salt and pepper. Place sliced eggs over meat. Cover with remaining rice mixture. Bake 25 to 30 minutes, or until thoroughly heated.

Venison Steaks or Chops

*8 venison steaks or chops, 1½ inches
 thick*
Dry red wine
Freshly ground pepper
Seasoned all-purpose flour

Butter
½ pound mushrooms, sliced
3 slices bacon, cut into small pieces
1 small onion, minced
½ cup diced celery

Place steaks or chops in a shallow dish and pour enough wine over the top to barely cover meat. Sprinkle liberally with pepper. Let stand overnight, turning occasionally. Remove steaks from marinade and pat dry. Dredge in seasoned flour. Heat enough butter in a large heavy skillet to cover the bottom. Add steaks and cook until browned on both sides and tender. While steaks are cooking, melt 2 tablespoons butter in another skillet. Add mushrooms, bacon, onion, and celery and cook slowly until onion is tender. Stir in about ¼ cup wine, bring to a boil, and simmer 2 minutes. Serve steaks topped with wine sauce.

Roast Venison with Sour Cream Gravy

3 cups dry red wine, divided
½ cup apple cider
3 bay leaves
4 whole peppercorns
1 6-pound venison roast

Salt
¼ cup butter
1½ tablespoons all-purpose flour
1 cup dairy sour cream

In a shallow dish combine 2½ cups wine with cider, bay leaves, and peppercorns. Place venison in wine mixture; cover and refrigerate overnight, turning occasionally. Preheat oven to 325°. Remove venison from marinade and place on a rack in a roasting pan, fat side up. Sprinkle with salt. Insert a meat thermometer in center of thickest part of meat, not touching bone or resting in fat. Melt butter in a small saucepan. Strain 1 cup of the marinade and add to butter. Brush meat with this mixture several times during roasting time. Roast meat to desired degree of doneness, approximately 25 minutes per pound for medium rare. Remove roast to a warm platter. In a 1½-quart saucepan combine flour and ½ teaspoon salt. Add ¾ cup drippings from the venison and stir until smooth. Stir in the remaining ½ cup wine. Cook over medium heat, stirring constantly, until smooth and thick. Reduce heat to low and stir in sour cream. Heat to serving temperature, but do not boil. Serve with venison.

IV
Fish and Shellfish

Fish and shellfish were a mainstay of the Early American diet, for they populated northern and southern waters in hundreds of varieties. Colonial cooks found hundreds of delicious ways to prepare them. Here is fish broiled, stuffed, fried, and baked—including the ever-popular Clambake—to entice modern appetites as they did hundreds of years ago. Today as always, the secret of the most appetite-appealing fish or shellfish, however prepared, is brevity. Long cooking makes shellfish tough and destroys its flavor; fish that is overcooked will fall to pieces.

Baked Striped Bass with Stuffed Clams

6 servings

20 littleneck clams, scrubbed and
   cleaned
1 whole striped bass (about 3 pounds),
   cleaned and boned
½ teaspoon salt, divided
⅛ teaspoon pepper, divided
½ cup butter, divided

½ cup finely chopped onions
1 clove garlic, crushed
⅓ cup fine dry bread crumbs
3 tablespoons minced parsley
Almondine Sauce
Lemon slices
Parsley sprigs

Place clams in a large saucepan. Add water to a depth of ¾ inch. Cover and bring to a boil; reduce heat to medium. Cook 5 to 7 minutes, or until clam shells are opened. Remove clams and set aside. Add enough water to broth to make 1⅓ cups; set aside. Preheat oven to 375°. Grease a large baking dish and place striped bass in it. Sprinkle fish inside and out with ¼ teaspoon salt and part of the pepper. Dot with ¼ cup butter. Pour 1 cup of the clam broth into baking dish. Bake fish 20 minutes. Meanwhile, remove clams from shells. Reserve 18 half shells; place in a shallow baking pan. Chop clams fine. Sauté onion and garlic in remaining butter. Add clams, bread crumbs, parsley, and remaining salt and pepper and mix well. Add enough broth to moisten. Spoon mixture into reserved half shells. When fish has baked 20 minutes, add stuffed clams to oven. Bake fish and clams 25 minutes, or until done, basting fish occasionally with liquid from bottom of pan. Fish is done when it flakes easily with a fork. Transfer fish to a warm serving platter. Pour on Almondine Sauce. Surround with hot stuffed clams. Garnish with lemon and parsley.

Almondine Sauce

Melt ¼ cup butter in a skillet over medium heat. Add ⅓ cup sliced almonds. Sauté, stirring, until almonds are golden.

Baked Bluefish

4 to 6 servings

1 3- to 4-pound bluefish
¼ pound salt pork
Salt and freshly ground pepper to
   taste

¼ cup butter
Milk
1 teaspoon chopped parsley

Preheat oven to 400°. Clean and wash fish, removing head and tail. Split fish and remove backbone. Wash in cold water and pat dry with paper towels. Slice salt pork in very thin slices and place in the bottom of a shallow baking dish large enough for the two pieces of fish. Lay fish skin side down on the salt pork. Sprinkle with salt and pepper and dot with butter. Pour enough milk over fish to completely cover bottom of the baking dish. Bake, basting occasionally, 45 minutes, or until fish flakes easily when tested with a fork. Sprinkle with parsley and serve with new potatoes.

Baked Shore Cod   *6 servings*

1 4- to 5-pound cod
Salt to taste
1 cup cracker crumbs
¼ teaspoon pepper
1 teaspoon salt
1 teaspoon minced onion

1 teaspoon chopped parsley
1 teaspoon chopped pickles
¼ cup finely chopped salt pork
½ cup heavy cream
Sliced salt pork

Preheat oven to 350°. Remove the fins, then scale and clean the cod. Rinse well with cold water and pat dry. Rub inside of fish with salt. Let stand 10 minutes. Combine next eight ingredients and toss lightly. Stuff fish with mixture. Sew opening, or close with wooden picks. Put a piece of aluminum foil in the bottom of a baking dish. Place cod on foil. Top fish with a few thin slices of salt pork. Bake 1 hour, or until fish flakes when tested with a fork.

Note: *Some colonial cooks liked to pour a cup of cold water around the fish before baking. This was used to baste the fish during baking; after the fish was cooked the liquid was thickened with a little flour and used for gravy.*

Codfish Rice Balls   *6 servings*

Salt and pepper to taste
1 pound fresh codfish fillets
½ cup minced onions
3 tablespoons butter
3 tablespoons all-purpose flour
½ cup milk
2 teaspoons salt

¼ teaspoon pepper
1 teaspoon dry mustard
2 cups cooked rice
2 teaspoons lemon juice
1 egg
Dry bread crumbs
Oil or fat for deep-frying

Season 1 quart water with salt and pepper to taste. Bring to a boil, add fish fillets, and simmer about 10 minutes, or until fish flakes easily when tested with a fork. Drain thoroughly. Flake fish and set aside. Cook onion in butter until soft but not browned. Blend in flour and cook 1 minute. Remove from heat and stir in milk, salt, pepper, and mustard. Cook, stirring constantly, until smooth and thickened. Remove from heat and fold in codfish, rice, and lemon juice. Chill mixture until thick, about 1 hour. Beat egg with 2 tablespoons water. Put bread crumbs in a flat dish. Shape codfish mixture into balls. Dip balls into egg mixture and roll in crumbs. Chill several hours. Heat fat or oil to 375°. Cook codfish balls in hot fat 3 to 4 minutes, or until browned and cooked through. Serve with tartar sauce or a sharp mustard sauce.

Salt Codfish Hash   *6 servings*

1½ pounds salt cod or other salt fish   *½ cup chopped onions*
¼ cup butter or lard, divided   *Freshly ground pepper*
4 cups cooked diced potatoes

Soak fish in lukewarm water until soft; depending on kind of fish used, this will take from 3 to 4 hours. Drain well and shred fish. There should be about 3 cups of shredded fish. Melt half the butter or lard in a large skillet. Combine fish, potatoes, onion, pepper, and ½ cup water in pan and stir until heated through. Push mixture to one side and melt remaining butter. Spread mixture over melted butter and press hash down evenly. Cook over medium heat until bottom is browned and crisp. Turn out on a heated platter and cut into wedges to serve. Serve with poached eggs, if desired.

Cape Cod Turkey   *5 to 6 servings*

1 pound salt cod   *2 cups milk*
¼ cup butter   *2 eggs, beaten*
¼ cup all-purpose flour   *¼ teaspoon pepper*

Soak codfish in cold water to cover overnight. Drain. Cover with fresh cold water and bring just to a boil. Drain well. Flake fish with a fork and set aside. Melt butter in top part of a double boiler. Blend in flour and cook, stirring, for 1 minute. Remove from heat. Stir in milk. Cook over medium heat, stirring constantly, until mixture thickens and comes to a boil. Stir a small amount of hot sauce into eggs, then return to white sauce. Place over boiling water. Add flaked codfish and pepper. Simmer over water until very hot. Serve over toast, mashed or baked potatoes, or rice.

Broiled New England Scrod   *6 servings*

1 3- to 3½-pound scrod   *2 tablespoons melted butter*
Salt and freshly ground pepper to   *Juice of ½ lemon*
*   taste*   *Chopped parsley*
3 to 4 tablespoons olive oil

Clean scrod and remove the head and tail. Split in half but do not separate halves. Remove backbone. Pat dry with paper towels. Sprinkle with salt and pepper and refrigerate for several hours or overnight. Preheat broiling compartment. Place fish, skin side down, on broiling pan. Brush with olive oil. Cook about 2 inches from source of heat about 15 minutes, or until fish flakes easily when tested with a fork. Place fish on a heated serving platter. Combine melted butter and lemon juice and pour over fish. Sprinkle with chopped parsley.

Codfish Cakes

6 servings

6 ounces salt cod
3 large potatoes
2 eggs

Salt and pepper to taste
Oil or fat for deep-frying

Wash fish in cold water. Cover with cold water in a kettle and bring to a boil. Drain, cover with cold water, and bring to a boil again. Repeat this process five or six times. Drain, cover with fresh water, and boil until the fish flakes apart easily. While codfish is cooking, peel and cook potatoes until tender. Drain potatoes and drain fish. Combine. Beat with an electric beater until light and smooth. Beat in eggs one at a time; season with salt and pepper to taste. Heat oil in a deep saucepan or deep-frying kettle to 370°. Drop mixture by spoonfuls into hot oil, making not more than six cakes at one time. When they are brown on one side, roll gently over to other side and brown. Remove with a slotted spoon and drain on absorbent paper. Repeat process, making about 18 cakes in all, three for each serving. Serve piping hot.

Baked Halibut

4 servings

1½ pounds sliced halibut
Salt and freshly ground pepper to
    taste

1 large ripe tomato
¼ cup butter

Preheat oven to 400°. Wash fish in cold water and pat dry with paper towels. Place in a well-buttered shallow baking dish. Sprinkle with salt and pepper. Peel tomato and cut in very thin slices. Place over top of fish. Dot with butter. Bake 25 minutes, basting occasionally with juice in the baking dish.

Connecticut River Planked Shad

6 servings

Clean a 3-pound shad and remove the head. Split the fish open and nail to a hardwood board. Set the board upright in front of an open fire. Broil until the fish is brown and cooked through, about 20 minutes. (Test for doneness by flaking with a fork.) Remove fish from plank. Spread with butter and season with salt and a bit of cayenne.

Maine Clam Fritters

4 servings

1 egg, separated
½ cup milk
1 tablespoon melted butter

⅛ teaspoon salt
½ cup sifted all-purpose flour
24 clams, shucked

Beat the egg yolk with milk, butter, and salt. Beat in flour. Beat egg white until stiff and fold into yolk batter. Drain clams thoroughly. Dip clams in batter and fry in hot fat until lightly browned on both sides.

Baked Connecticut River Shad

4 to 6 servings

1 shad, cleaned and split
1½ teaspoons salt
1 teaspoon pepper

¼ cup butter
Chopped parsley
1 or 2 lemons

Preheat oven to 400°. Wash shad and pat dry. Place in a well-greased baking dish. Sprinkle with salt and pepper. Dot with butter. Bake 25 to 30 minutes, or until fish flakes easily when tested with a fork. Sprinkle with parsley and serve with lemon wedges.

Connecticut Stuffed Baked Shad

6 servings

1 cup cracker crumbs
¼ cup melted butter
¼ teaspoon salt
¼ teaspoon pepper
1 small onion, minced

1 teaspoon sage
1 5-pound shad, split and boned, head
  and tail left on
¼ pound sliced bacon

Preheat oven to 400°. Combine cracker crumbs, butter, salt, pepper, onion, and sage and toss lightly. Stuff shad with mixture and sew edges of fish together. Place on a rack in a baking pan. Pour in about ½ cup hot water. Cover top of fish with bacon strips and fasten down with toothpicks. Bake 10 minutes. Reduce heat to 325° and continue baking about 35 minutes, or until done, basting frequently. Remove one bacon strip and test fish with a fork to see if it flakes easily; if not, return to oven and bake 5 minutes more. Serve on a hot platter.

Broiled Shad Roe

Dip shad roe in melted butter and lay on a greased broiler rack. Broil about 4 inches from source of heat for 8 to 10 minutes, turning once and brushing several times with melted butter. Season with salt and pepper. Serve with strips of crisp bacon and more melted butter.

Fish Soufflé

4 to 6 servings

¾ pound fillet of flounder
1 carrot, peeled and chopped
1 medium onion, quartered
1 stalk celery, cut up
¾ teaspoon salt
6 peppercorns

¼ cup butter
½ cup unsifted all-purpose flour
1 cup milk
5 eggs, separated
2 tablespoons minced parsley
1 teaspoon grated lemon peel

Preheat oven to 350°. Combine fish, carrot, onion, celery, salt, peppercorns, and 2 cups water in a saucepan. Bring mixture to a boil; reduce heat and simmer until fish flakes easily with a fork, about 6 minutes. Strain mixture, reserving liquid. Return liquid to saucepan and boil until reduced to 2 cups. Flake fish fine and set aside. Discard vegetables and spices. Melt butter in a large saucepan. Remove from heat and blend in flour. Return to heat and cook, stirring, for 1 minute. Remove from heat. Stir in milk and reserved fish liquid, blending well. Cook over medium heat, stirring constantly, until mixture comes to a boil. Remove from heat and fold in flaked fish. Beat egg yolks thoroughly. Stir 1 cup of the fish mixture into egg yolks; blend well. Stir into remaining mixture in saucepan. Stir in parsley and lemon peel. Beat egg whites until stiff but not dry. Fold into fish mixture. Turn into an ungreased 2-quart soufflé dish. Run spatula around mixture in a circle 1 inch deep and about 1 inch from edge of dish. Bake 45 to 50 minutes, or until set. Serve immediately.

Shad Roe with Bacon   *1 serving*

1 pair shad roe	*3 whole allspice*
1 small onion, sliced	*1 bay leaf*
1 teaspoon cider vinegar	*1 teaspoon salt*
6 peppercorns	*4 slices bacon*

Place shad roe in a heavy skillet. Add onion, vinegar, peppercorns, allspice, bay leaf, and salt. Cover with boiling water. Cover and simmer 5 minutes. Remove from heat and let stand for 10 minutes. In another skillet fry bacon until crisp and brown. Remove bacon and reserve. Lift roe from water and drain thoroughly. Fry roe in hot bacon fat until lightly browned and crisp on both sides. Season to taste and serve with bacon.

Fried Eels

Eels were in abundance—and much appreciated—everywhere along the coast when the colonists settled the land. Many people today seem to dislike eel, but when it is prepared and set before them, they appreciate it. There are still a great many eels along the coast of Connecticut and Rhode Island, located in tidal streams and bays. Most people's prejudice against eels is because of their serpentlike appearance.

Skin the eels and let stand in boiling water for a few minutes. Cut eels into 3-inch lengths. Roll in a mixture of flour and cornmeal. Pan-fry in hot fat until brown on all sides. Allow about ½ pound eel for each serving.

To skin an eel: Cut through the skin all around just back of the head. Grasp the skin with a pair of pliers, hold the head in one hand, and pull off the skin with the other. It needs a tough, hard pull, but once the knack is acquired it is simple. Slit the belly from vent to throat, remove the intestines, and cut off the head—and the eel is cleaned. Then cut the fish into lengths for frying or using in chowders. If you wish to fillet the eels, cut the cleaned eels into 6-inch lengths and chill for about an hour. This firms the meat and makes it easier to remove the bones. With a small, very sharp knife make a cut from the eel's back, right next to the backbone, down to the rib case. Holding this cut open with your thumb, cut the fillet loose from the rib case, using a series of shallow cuts made with the very point of the knife. Cut fillets into 1-inch chunks.

Fish Fry

1 pound fish fillets
1 egg
2 tablespoons milk

¼ teaspoon salt
½ cup fine dry bread crumbs
2 cups cooking oil

Wipe fish fillets with a damp cloth or paper towel. Combine egg, milk, and salt and beat until blended. Dip fish in egg mixture and roll in crumbs. Heat oil in a skillet to 375° on a deep-fat thermometer. Fry fish until golden brown on both sides. Drain fish on absorbent paper.

Martha's Vineyard Eel Stifle

4 cups thinly sliced potatoes
4 onions, thinly sliced
2 pounds eels

Salt and pepper to taste
All-purpose flour
¼ pound salt pork, diced

Place a layer of potatoes and onion in the bottom of a heavy kettle. Slice eels in small pieces and place a layer of eels on top of potatoes. Sprinkle with salt, pepper, and flour. Continue making layers until all potatoes, onion, and eels are in the kettle. Fry the salt pork until browned. Pour pork bits and fat over top of layers. Add enough hot water to almost cover layers. Cover tightly and simmer 45 to 55 minutes, or until tender.

Fried Smelts

Clean, wash, and dry smelts. Roll in flour that has been seasoned with salt and pepper. Beat together 1 egg and 2 tablespoons water. Dip fish in egg mixture, then roll in cornmeal. Melt fat or butter in a heavy skillet. Pan-fry smelts in hot fat until they are evenly browned on both sides and cooked through. Serve with tartar sauce, if desired.

Boiled Live Lobster

Fill a large kettle with sufficient water to cover lobsters and add 1 tablespoon of salt for each quart of water. Unless very large kettles are available, standard-size pots will hold 2 to 3 lobsters, depending on weight. Bring water to a full rolling boil. Grasp lobster at the back of the head, just behind the claws, and plunge head first into boiling water. Bring back to a boil and simmer 5 minutes for the first pound of lobster and 3 minutes for each additional pound. Remove from water and place on a board to drain. (If you snip the end of each large claw with kitchen scissors and hold up the lobster, much of the water will drain out.) Place lobster on its back. With a heavy knife split it in half from head to tail. Remove the stomach and intestinal tract. Keep the green liver (called tomalley) and any reddish deposit—the roe or coral. Serve either hot or cold with hot melted butter or mayonnaise.

Salmon *in* Cases.

CUT your Salmon into little Pieces, such as will lay rolled in Half Sheets of Paper; season it with Pepper, Salt and Nutmeg, butter the Inside of the Paper well, fold the Paper so as nothing can come out, then lay them on a Tin Plate to be baked, pour a little melted Butter over the Papers, and then Crumbs of Bread all over them. Don't let your Oven be too hot, for fear of burning the Paper; a Tin Oven before the Fire does best. When you think they are enough, serve them up just as they are; there will be Sauce enough in the Papers.

Salmon in Cases   *4 servings*

4 salmon steaks   4 tablespoons butter, divided
Salt and pepper to taste   ½ cup dry bread crumbs, divided
Pinch of ground nutmeg

Preheat oven to 400°. Tear off four squares of aluminum foil. Place one salmon steak in the center of each piece of foil. Sprinkle with salt, pepper, and nutmeg. Put 1 tablespoon butter and 2 tablespoons bread crumbs on top of each steak. Make a drugstore fold over the top of fish and fold edges up over fold. Place packages on a baking sheet. Bake 15 minutes. Remove 1 package and test fish to see if it flakes easily with a fork. If not, return fish and bake 5 more minutes, or until it is done.

Note: *This recipe proves that there is nothing new under the sun—except perhaps for aluminum foil, which we have substituted for the parchment paper originally called for. Cooking food wrapped-up in cases is certainly not new. Be sure to use a healthy pinch of nutmeg, for it gives the fish a unique and quite pleasant taste.*

Fried Soft-Shell Crabs

6 servings

12 soft-shell crabs

Salt and pepper to taste

All-purpose flour

¼ cup butter

Clean crabs thoroughly and pat dry. Sprinkle with salt and pepper. Dust very lightly with flour. Melt butter in a heavy skillet. Fry crabs until lightly browned, about 5 minutes on each side. Serve with tartar sauce, if desired.

Deviled Crab Meat

4 servings

4 tablespoons butter, divided

½ cup finely chopped onions

¾ cup (about) fine soft
* bread crumbs, divided*

1 cup heavy cream

¼ teaspoon cayenne

½ teaspoon dry mustard

Hot pepper sauce

2 egg yolks, beaten

Salt to taste

1 pound lump crab meat, picked over
* to remove bits of shell*

Preheat oven to 375°. Melt 2 tablespoons butter in a skillet. Add onion and cook until soft but not browned. Add ½ cup bread crumbs, cream, cayenne, and mustard. Add hot pepper sauce to taste. Stir in egg yolks. Add salt to taste. Gently fold in crab meat. Divide mixture among four buttered ramekins or shells. Dot with remaining butter. Sprinkle about 1 teaspoon soft bread crumbs on top of each ramekin. Bake 10 to 13 minutes, or until piping hot and golden brown on top.

Broiled Live Lobster

Split the lobster lengthwise. Remove the stomach and the intestinal tract. Crack the lobster claws and lay the lobster out as flat as possible. Place on broiler pan, shell side down. Brush with melted butter. Place in broiler about 6 inches from source of heat and broil until shell turns red and flesh becomes white and opaque. Brush occasionally with more melted butter while cooking. Serve with hot melted butter. Allow ½ large lobster or 1 small lobster per serving.

To split lobster: Place live lobster on its back with the large claws over its head. Insert the point of a very sharp knife just under the mouth and with a quick motion draw the knife down the whole length of the body, splitting the lobster into 2 halves. Open the body and remove the intestinal vein, liver, roe, and stomach, which is located just under the head. Save liver and roe. Crack claws. You can also ask the fish dealer to split the lobster for you.

Clam Cakes   *4 servings*

1 quart clams, shucked   *2 eggs, well beaten*
½ cup clam liquor   *Oil or fat for deep-frying*
1 cup (about) fine cracker crumbs

Drain and pick over clams. Reserve liquor. Remove the black from soft
part of clam. Put the necks of the clams through a food chopper. Put clams
and necks in a bowl; add clam liquor and enough crumbs to absorb all
moisture. Let stand 10 minutes. Add eggs and mix well. Shape mixture
into flat, thick cakes. Heat fat to 375°. Place cakes in hot fat and cook until
golden brown on both sides. Drain on absorbent paper.

Clambake

The basis of a real New England clambake is of course clams and lobsters.
However, the menu can vary, depending on the taste of the crowd and the
availability of any item. For fifteen people, ½ bushel of soft-shell clams
is enough. There should be at least 1 lobster per person, ½ chicken per
person, corn on the cob, 1 or 2 sweet or white potatoes, and, if desired,
whole onions and some kind of flat fish. These are usually bagged in cheesecloth for a large party so that they are easy to handle. For dessert, provide
enough cold watermelon to go around and plenty of hot coffee.

Dig a large hole or pit, about 3 feet in diameter and 1 to 2 feet deep.
Line the pit with large, dry rocks and over this build a large roaring fire.
Allow 2 to 3 hours for the fire to burn down to ash and then rake the ash
away. Put a thick layer of wet seaweed on the hot rocks. Quickly now, a
cheesecloth bag of clams goes on the seaweed, bagged chicken halves that
have been browned just a little on a grill, fresh husked corn, potatoes and
onions, if desired, the flat fish, which is also bagged, and last of all a layer
of lobsters. Cover with a layer of seaweed and place a large tarpaulin over
the top. Anchor the edges of the tarpaulin with large rocks and a layer of
sand to keep the steam inside the pit.

Allow this to steam from 1 to 2 hours. The easiest way to check is to lift a
corner of the tarpaulin and remove a lobster or chicken to test for doneness.
It is usual to eat the clams first, with plenty of melted butter, then progress
to the lobster and other foods, again served with lots of melted butter. Some
people serve cold beer with the meal, or you may offer any drink you wish.
At the end comes the traditional cold, juicy watermelon and the coffee.

Note: *The first clambake, by the method the Indians taught the settlers, had just
pit-baked clams—nothing else. The savory extras were added one by one, perhaps
because it seemed a shame to waste all that precious cooking heat on clams alone.*

Scalloped Oysters

4 servings

½ cup fresh bread crumbs
1 cup cracker crumbs
¼ cup butter, melted
1 pint oysters, drained, liquor
    reserved

Salt and pepper to taste
2 cups light cream, divided

Preheat oven to 400°. Grease a shallow baking dish. Combine bread crumbs, cracker crumbs, and melted butter. Put a thin layer of crumbs in bottom of the dish. Cover with a layer of half the oysters. Sprinkle with salt, pepper, and 2 tablespoons oyster liquor. Add 1 cup cream. Make a second layer of crumbs and the remaining oysters, liquor, and cream. Cover top with a layer of remaining crumbs. Bake 20 minutes, or until piping hot and lightly browned on top.

Oyster Tricorns

50 small turnovers

25 oysters, well drained
⅛ teaspoon freshly ground pepper
¼ teaspoon whole celery seed

1 cup sifted all-purpose flour
¼ teaspoon ground nutmeg
½ cup butter

Cut each oyster in half. Toss with black pepper and celery seed; set aside. Sift flour and nutmeg together. Cut in butter with pastry blender or two knives until butter is the size of peas. Add 1 tablespoon water and mix just enough to hold dough together. Shape into a ball and chill until it handles easily, about 1 hour. Preheat oven to 425°. Roll pastry out to about ⅛-inch thickness on a lightly floured board. Cut into 1½-inch squares. Place half an oyster slightly off center of each square. Fold pastry over. Seal edges and crimp with a fork. Place on baking sheets. Bake 7 to 9 minutes, or until lightly browned.

Charleston Shrimp Bake

4 to 6 servings

¼ cup butter
¼ cup fine dry bread crumbs
1½ cups chopped green pepper
¼ cup chopped onion
4 cups dry bread cubes

1½ teaspoons salt
⅛ teaspoon pepper
1 can (1 pound) tomatoes
1½ pounds uncooked medium shrimp,
    shelled and deveined

Preheat oven to 350°. Melt butter in a large skillet. Remove 1 tablespoon of the butter and mix thoroughly with the dry bread crumbs. Set aside. Add green pepper and onion to butter in skillet. Cook over medium heat, stirring occasionally, until tender, about 5 minutes. Mix in bread cubes, salt, pepper, tomatoes, and shrimp. Turn mixture into a 2-quart oblong baking dish. Sprinkle with buttered bread crumbs. Bake 25 to 30 minutes, or until shrimp are tender.

V
Vegetables

Squash, pumpkins, corn, sweet potatoes, beans of many kinds—the New World added many new vegetables to the repertoire of the colonial cook. Southern women tended to cook vegetables longer than northern cooks did, and to embellish them more, as with the piece of salt pork or fatback that often went into the pot in which green beans were cooked. North or South, vegetables were cooked much longer in early times than we have more recently learned to enjoy them. Another recent pleasure is year-round availability of most vegetables. Originally, those that could not be stored for the winter were eaten only in the growing season. Today your delighted family and guests can sample present-day versions of traditional favorites whatever the season.

Black-Eyed Peas   *6 servings*

1 pound dried black-eyed peas
1½ pounds smoked boneless pork
  shoulder butt or 1 ham bone

1 large onion, diced
1 teaspoon salt
¼ cup dry white wine (optional)

Pick over peas, discarding any that are soft or spoiled. Cover with cold water and let soak overnight. Drain peas and put in a large pot with pork, onion, and salt. Add 2 quarts water. Bring to a boil. Lower heat, cover, and simmer about 2 hours, or until peas are tender. Stir occasionally during cooking time and add more boiling water, about ½ cup, if peas dry out. When ready to serve, taste, and add more salt if necessary. Stir in wine and serve peas immediately.

Hopping John   *6 servings*

2 cups dried black-eyed peas

½ pound bacon, in one piece

1 teaspoon salt

1 cup long-grained rice

Pick over peas. Cover with cold water and let soak overnight. Put bacon in a kettle with 2 quarts water, bring to a boil, and simmer about 1 hour. Add drained peas and salt and return to a boil. Continue cooking gently about 30 minutes, or until peas are almost tender. Add rice, bring to a boil, and simmer 15 to 20 minutes, or until rice is tender. Remove bacon and reserve. Drain peas and rice and put in a warm oven for a few minutes until rice is fluffy. Slice the bacon and serve with the peas and rice, along with hot corn bread and butter.

Vermont Baked Beans   *6 servings*

3 cups pea beans
½ pound salt pork
¾ cup maple syrup

3 tablespoons sugar
2 teaspoons dry mustard
1 teaspoon salt

Pick over beans. Cover with cold water and let soak overnight. Drain; place in a kettle, cover with water, and bring slowly to a boil. Lower heat, cover, and simmer about 2 hours, or until tender. To test for tenderness, remove a few beans from the kettle with a spoon, and blow on them; if the skins burst, the beans are cooked. While beans are cooking, cover salt pork with boiling water and let stand 5 minutes. Remove; cut in two pieces and score the rind. Preheat oven to 300°. Put one piece of salt pork in the bottom of a bean pot. Drain cooked beans and pour into bean pot. Combine maple syrup, sugar, mustard, and salt. Blend with 1 cup boiling water and pour over beans. Bury second piece of salt pork in top of beans, leaving rind exposed. Add enough additional boiling water just to cover beans. Cover pot and bake about 8 hours. If beans dry out, add more boiling water during cooking period. About 30 minutes before beans are cooked, remove lid so that top of beans and pork can brown.

Boston Baked Beans
8 to 10 servings

Many a Massachusetts household would consider a Saturday night supper that lacked codfish cakes and baked beans as approaching heresy. The tradition began in colonial times and still holds good today.

1 quart pea beans	1/3 cup molasses
1/2 pound salt pork	1 teaspoon salt
1 very small onion	1/2 teaspoon dry mustard
1/3 cup brown sugar	

Cover beans with cold water and let soak overnight. Drain off water and put beans in a kettle. Cover with cold water; bring to a boil. Lower heat and simmer until beans are cooked. Test by removing a few beans in a spoon and blowing on them. If skins crack, it is time to take the beans off the heat. Preheat oven to 300°. Cut a thin slice of salt pork and place in bottom of bean pot. Score rind of remaining salt pork. Place 2 cups beans in bean pot and bury onion in beans. Fill pot with remaining beans. Bury salt pork in beans, leaving rind exposed. Combine remaining ingredients with 1/2 cup hot water. Pour over top of beans. Add enough boiling water to cover beans. Cover pot and bake 6 to 8 hours. If beans dry out, add more water during cooking period. Remove cover from top of bean pot during last hour of cooking to brown skin of salt pork.

Maple Baked Carrots
4 to 6 servings

4 large carrots, peeled and sliced	2 tablespoons brown sugar
2 medium apples	2 tablespoons butter
2 tablespoons maple syrup	

Preheat oven to 375°. Cook carrots in a small amount of boiling salted water 20 minutes, or just until tender. Grease a 1½-quart baking dish. Drain carrots. Peel, core, and thinly slice the apples. Place carrots and apples in baking dish. Pour maple syrup and brown sugar over the top. Dot with butter. Bake 30 to 40 minutes, or until apples are tender, stirring once or twice during cooking period.

Mashed Carrots and Parsnips
4 servings

4 large carrots	1 teaspoon sugar
6 large fresh parsnips	2 tablespoons butter
1/2 teaspoon salt	

Peel carrots and slice in rounds. Wash and peel parsnips and split in two lengthwise. Split in quarters and cut out the pithy core. Cut in slices. Place carrots and parsnips in a saucepan with salt, sugar, and water to cover. Bring to a boil and cook about 30 minutes, or until tender. Drain well. Mash with a potato masher; add butter and beat until well blended. Reheat over boiling water, if necessary, before serving.

Jerusalem Artichokes

4 to 6 servings

1½ pounds Jerusalem artichokes
⅓ cup melted butter
3 tablespoons fresh lemon juice

½ teaspoon salt
Few sprigs parsley, chopped

Peel artichokes and cook in boiling salted water until tender. Test with a toothpick or wooden skewer after about 15 minutes; artichokes should not be overcooked. Drain thoroughly. Toss with butter, lemon juice, salt, and some chopped parsley.

Baked Corn

3 to 4 servings

½ cup butter, divided
12 large ears corn
¾ teaspoon salt

Generous grind of pepper
½ tablespoon sugar

Preheat oven to 375°. Spread a 9-inch ovenproof glass pie plate with a thick layer of butter. Husk the corn. Remove corn from the cob with a sharp knife, cutting only about half the depth of the kernels. With the back of the knife scrape out the rest of the pulp. Season corn with salt, pepper, and sugar and put in the buttered pie plate. Dot with butter. Bake 40 to 45 minutes, or until the top is a crusty golden brown.

Fried Corn

8 to 10 servings

Remove corn from the cob with a sharp knife, cutting only about half the depth of the kernels. With the back of the knife scrape out the rest of the pulp. Cut enough to make about 5 cups of cut corn. Put ⅓ cup bacon fat and about 2 tablespoons butter in a heavy skillet. Heat fat, add corn, and stir briskly for 1 minute. Add just enough water to make a gravylike mixture. Season to taste with salt and pepper. Cook 5 minutes, stirring constantly. Reduce heat to very low, cover skillet tightly, and simmer 20 minutes, stirring occasionally. The mixture should be thick when ready to serve.

Greens, Southern Style

6 to 8 servings

3 pounds mustard greens, turnip
   greens, or collard greens
1 onion, diced

½ pound salt pork or unsliced bacon
Salt to taste

Trim greens and discard hard stems. Wash greens in several changes of cold water. Put in a large pot. Add 2 cups water, onion, salt pork, and salt to taste. Bring to a boil. Lower heat, cover, and simmer about 1 hour, or until greens are very tender. Taste and add more salt if necessary. Serve with sliced salt pork or bacon and hot corn bread.

Young Greens with Bacon Dressing — *6 servings*

4 slices bacon, diced
½ cup sugar
½ teaspoon salt
1 tablespoon cornstarch
1 egg, lightly beaten
¼ cup cider vinegar

1 cup light cream
4 cups young tender dandelion greens
  or new garden lettuce, cleaned and
  dried
1 hard-cooked egg, chopped

Cook the bacon until crisp. Combine sugar, salt, and cornstarch. Combine egg, vinegar, and cream and blend well. Stir into sugar mixture. Pour into cooked bacon with drippings. Cook over medium heat, stirring constantly, until mixture thickens. Pour over greens, tossing lightly. Garnish with hard-cooked egg and serve immediately, while dressing is still warm.

Wilted Salad — *6 servings*

1 head iceberg lettuce or 1½ pounds
  fresh spinach
1 small onion, minced
3 slices bacon
¼ cup vinegar

2 tablespoons cooking oil
½ teaspoon salt
¼ teaspoon pepper
½ teaspoon prepared mustard
1 teaspoon sugar (optional)

Wash lettuce or spinach and pat dry. Break in small pieces in a glass or pottery bowl. Add onion, toss lightly and refrigerate. Cut bacon in small pieces. Fry until crisp and brown. Add vinegar, oil, salt, pepper, mustard, and sugar, if desired; heat thoroughly. Pour hot dressing over chilled greens and serve immediately.

Variation: Use sour cream instead of cooking oil.

Baked Onion Rings — *4 servings*

6 medium or large onions
1 tablespoon all-purpose flour
Freshly ground pepper to taste
3 tablespoons butter

1 cup milk
1 teaspoon salt
Chopped parsley

Preheat over to 450°. Peel and slice onions very thin. Separate into rings. Toss with flour. Place in a deep baking dish. Sprinkle lightly with pepper. Dot with butter and pour milk over top. Bake about 45 minutes, or until onions are tender. Sprinkle with salt and parsley and serve.

Glazed Onions

4 *servings*

10 *medium onions*
10 *teaspoons honey*
1/4 *cup butter*

1/2 *teaspoon salt*
1/4 *teaspoon pepper*

Preheat oven to 450°. Peel onions and cut in half crosswise. Arrange in a baking dish. Pour honey carefully over tops of onions. Dot with butter and season with salt and pepper. Bake 45 minutes, or until onions are glazed and tender, spooning some of the syrup over the tops of the onions from time to time during cooking.

Hominy Grits

4 *servings*

1 *cup hominy grits*
1 *teaspoon salt*

1 *tablespoon butter*

Pour grits slowly into 4 cups boiling salted water, stirring constantly. Continue stirring until mixture boils. Lower heat and simmer gently, stirring frequently, for 1 hour. Add butter and stir lightly. Serve hot with butter or gravy.

Herbed Spinach

4 *servings*

2 *pounds spinach*
1/4 *teaspoon fresh rosemary or*
  large pinch of dried rosemary
3 *sprigs parsley, chopped*

1 *scallion, cleaned and chopped*
2 *tablespoons butter*
Salt and pepper to taste

Wash spinach several times in tepid water to remove sand. Remove thick stems and discard. Chop spinach coarsely and pile in a large saucepan. Add remaining ingredients with only the water that clings to the spinach. Bring to a boil and simmer, covered, about 5 minutes, or just until spinach is limp but still bright in color. Toss lightly and serve immediately.

Resin-Baked Potatoes

In the pine belts of Florida and Georgia, where resin flows from the trees, potatoes are baked in resin in huge cast-iron pots. The cooking is usually done outdoors, but can be done indoors, if great care is taken. Place resin in an old cast-iron pot or dutch oven, filling about half full. Heat to boiling. Carefully lower scrubbed and dried baking potatoes into kettle with a long-handled spoon. Let potatoes boil until they rise to the surface. As each potato is done, place it on a 1-foot square of brown paper. Fold paper over in a double fold at top and sides to enclose potato; this will keep potato hot while others are cooking. Serve with salt, pepper, and lots of butter. Keep the resin stored in the pot for other cookouts.

Summer Succotash

4 servings

2 cups shelled shell beans
1 small onion, peeled
1 thick slice bacon, cut in pieces
2 cups fresh corn cut from
  the cob

½ teaspoon salt
Freshly ground pepper to taste
½ cup heavy cream

Put the beans, onion, bacon, and about 3 cups of water in a heavy saucepan. Bring to a boil, lower heat, cover, and simmer about 2 hours, or until tender. Check during cooking time and add more water if necessary. Add the corn, salt, and pepper. Bring to a boil, lower heat, and simmer about 5 minutes more, or until corn is tender. Remove from heat and stir in the cream just before serving.

Succotash

6 servings

2 thin slices salt pork
2 pounds fresh lima beans, shelled
8 ears corn
1 large ripe tomato, skinned and cut in
  cubes

1 teaspoon salt
¼ teaspoon pepper
Dash of ground nutmeg

Lay slices of salt pork in bottom of a saucepan and cover with lima beans. Add enough water to cover. Cook over low heat until beans are tender. Cut kernels from corn cobs and combine with beans, tomato, and seasonings. Cover and continue cooking over low heat 10 to 15 minutes, stirring frequently to prevent mixture from scorching.

Century Summer Succotash

8 servings

2 pounds young green beans
2 thick slices bacon, cut in pieces
12 ears corn

1 teaspoon salt
2 tablespoons butter
Freshly ground pepper to taste

Rinse green beans in cold water and break in 1-inch pieces. Place in a saucepan with bacon pieces. Add about ½ cup water and simmer 10 to 12 minutes, or until beans are tender. Cut the kernels from the corn cobs and add to the beans with the salt. Cook about 10 minutes longer, or until beans and corn are tender. Add butter and pepper and serve.

Baked Turnips with Maple Sugar   *6 servings*

5 to 6 cups grated yellow
   turnips
1 medium apple, peeled, cored, and
   diced

2 tablespoons maple sugar
1 teaspoon salt
¼ teaspoon pepper
3 tablespoons butter, melted

Preheat oven to 350°. Grease a 1½-quart baking dish. Combine turnip and diced apples. Stir in maple sugar, salt, pepper, and butter. Mix thoroughly. Turn into baking dish. Bake 1½ hours.

Rutabagas and Potatoes   *6 servings*

3 small rutabagas, peeled
   and cut in cubes
Salt to taste

2 large potatoes, peeled
   and cut in cubes
¼ cup light cream, warmed
3 tablespoons butter

Place rutabagas in a large saucepan. Cover with cold water, add salt, and bring to a boil. Lower heat and cook 30 minutes, or until almost tender. Add potatoes. Continue cooking 20 to 30 minutes, or until both potatoes and rutabagas are tender. Drain thoroughly. Mash with a potato masher or an electric beater. Beat in warm cream and butter and more salt if necessary. Whip thoroughly and serve piping hot.

Harvard Beets   *4 servings*

1½ teaspoons cornstarch
¼ cup sugar
¼ teaspoon salt
Pinch of pepper

½ cup cider vinegar
2 cups thinly sliced cooked beets
1 tablespoon butter

Combine cornstarch, sugar, salt, and pepper. Add vinegar and ¼ cup water and stir well. Bring to a boil over medium heat and cook until sauce is clear and thickened. Add beets and simmer over low heat just until beets are piping hot. Stir in butter and serve.

Bourbon Sweet Potatoes   *8 servings*

4 pounds sweet potatoes or yams
½ cup butter, melted
½ cup bourbon
⅓ cup orange juice

¼ cup firmly packed brown sugar
1 teaspoon salt
½ teaspoon apple-pie spice
½ cup chopped pecans

Scrub potatoes. Cook in boiling salted water to cover about 35 minutes, or just until tender. Drain; cool slightly and peel. Preheat oven to 350°. Grease a 6-cup baking dish. Place potatoes in a large bowl and whip with an electric beater. Add butter, bourbon, orange juice, brown sugar, salt, and apple-pie spice. Beat until fluffy. Spoon mixture into baking dish. Sprinkle nuts over top. Bake 45 minutes, or until hot and lightly browned.

Carolina Red Rice

6 to 7 servings

8 slices bacon
1 large onion, finely chopped
1 can (6 ounces) tomato paste
1 tablespoon salt

¼ teaspoon pepper
Pinch of thyme
2 cups long-grained rice

Cook bacon until crisp. Remove and drain on absorbent paper. Pour most of bacon fat into a heatproof measuring cup; reserve. Add onion to remaining small amount of fat in skillet and cook until soft but not browned. Add tomato paste, 1½ cups water, salt, pepper, and thyme. Stir well. Put rice in top part of a large double boiler. Add sauce, which should measure 2 cups. Add ½ cup bacon fat; if there is not enough, add butter. Crumble cooked bacon and add to mixture. Cover tightly and cook over boiling water 50 to 60 minutes, or until rice is tender and all liquid absorbed.

Baked Winter Squash

4 servings

1 pound winter squash
¼ cup butter
½ cup firmly packed light brown sugar

½ teaspoon salt
Freshly ground pepper to taste

Preheat oven to 375°. Wash squash and split open. Remove seeds and peel. Cut into cubes about 1 inch square. Place in a baking dish in layers, dotting each layer with butter and brown sugar. Sprinkle salt and pepper on top. Pour ¼ cup cold water over squash. Bake 1 hour, or until squash is tender, stirring gently once or twice during cooking period.

Baked Acorn Squash

6 servings

3 large acorn squash
6 teaspoons butter
6 teaspoons brown sugar

Salt
Ground cinnamon

Preheat oven to 350°. Wash the squash and split in halves. Remove seeds and strings in cavity. Place cut side down on a large shallow baking pan. Bake 45 minutes, or until tender. Cut a small piece off each curved side of squash, then turn each one over with the hollowed side up. Place a teaspoon of butter and a teaspoon of brown sugar in center of each squash half. Sprinkle lightly with salt and cinnamon. Bake 15 minutes longer, or until lightly browned on top.

Variation: For a delicious change of flavor, substitute maple sugar for the brown sugar in this recipe. Or use maple syrup, 2 teaspoons for each squash half.

Dried Corn

1 cup dried corn

2 teaspoons sugar

½ teaspoon salt

2 tablespoons butter

½ cup light cream

Place corn in a saucepan. Cover with 2 cups boiling water and let stand for at least 1 hour, preferably 2 hours. Add sugar, salt, and butter. Bring to a boil over moderate heat; lower heat and cook, covered, about 30 minutes. Stir occasionally during cooking period to keep corn from scorching. Stir in cream and simmer 3 to 4 minutes. Serve hot.

Sweet and Sour Red Cabbage

6 servings

1 onion, chopped

3 tablespoons shortening or bacon
    drippings

9 cups shredded red cabbage

2 tart apples, peeled, cored, and diced

3 tablespoons cider vinegar

3 tablespoons brown sugar

1¼ teaspoons salt

¼ teaspoon pepper

¼ cup seedless raisins (optional)

Cook onion in hot shortening until tender but not browned. Add cabbage, cover, and simmer 3 to 4 minutes. Add remaining ingredients with 1 cup water. Bring to a boil. Reduce heat, cover, and simmer about 10 minutes, or until cabbage is tender.

VI
Desserts

From the humble to the elegant, early Americans loved sweets. A "dessert table"—a handsomely arranged service of many kinds of sweet dishes, including pies and pastries, puddings, preserves, sweetmeats, and some things that we would no longer find acceptable, such as veal in a vanilla-custard sauce—was considered the truly stylish refreshment to serve after an evening's entertainment of music or dancing. Here are well-known and lesser-known favorites: puddings and pies, cakes and cookies, often spiked with the lively taste of cinnamon, nutmeg, and mace. One of Martha Washington's cake recipes begins, "Take 40 eggs," but the desserts you will find in this section have been tailored for modern kitchens—and modern appetites.

Party Apples   8 to 10 servings

12 apples   1 cup quince jelly
3 cups sugar   ½ cup brandy, warmed

Select perfect cooking apples, all the same size. Peel and core apples. Combine sugar with 2 cups water in a saucepan and bring to a boil. Add apples and simmer gently until apples are tender but still whole and firm. Place apples in a shallow serving dish. Fill centers with jelly. Boil down the syrup in the saucepan until very thick. Pour over the apples. Just before serving, pour warmed brandy over apples and ignite with a wooden match.

Bean-Pot Applesauce

Preheat oven to 250°. Peel, quarter, and core cooking apples. Put apples in a bean pot. For every 8 apples, combine ½ cup sugar and ½ teaspoon ground cinnamon. Sprinkle over layers of apples. Cover with sweet cider and bake 2 to 3 hours, or until fruit is tender but still holds its shape.

Apple Brown Betty   6 servings

A Betty used ingredients that came readily to hand in early times—the abundant fruit, and leftover bread that might otherwise grow too stale to put on the table. There were other Bettys, too, notably rhubarb and blueberry.

4 cups large bread crumbs   Pinch of salt
½ cup melted butter   ¾ cup brown sugar
¾ teaspoon ground cinnamon   4 cups chopped cooking apples

Grease a 1½-quart baking dish. Preheat oven to 375°. Combine bread crumbs with butter, cinnamon, salt, and sugar and toss lightly. Make alternate layers of crumb mixture and apples in baking dish, ending with bread crumbs. Bake about 1 hour, or until top is a rich golden brown and apples are tender. Serve warm with heavy cream.

Apple Tapioca   6 servings

¼ cup pearl tapioca   5 cooking apples
¼ teaspoon salt   ½ cup sugar

Soak tapioca in 2 cups water for several hours or overnight. Turn into a saucepan and cook 20 minutes or until tapioca is transparent. Add salt. Preheat oven to 350°. Peel apples and cut in quarters, removing cores. Place in a baking dish, and sprinkle with sugar. Pour tapioca over apples. Bake 45 minutes, or until apples are tender.

Charleston Apple Charlotte

6 servings

3 tablespoons butter
6 slices white bread
3 large baking apples, peeled, cored,
  and thinly sliced
Sugar

½ cup orange juice
1 tablespoon lemon juice
½ cup orange marmalade
3 egg whites, at room temperature

Preheat oven to 350°. Spread butter on bread and cut each slice into quarters. Grease a 2-quart oblong baking dish and line the bottom with half the apples. Sprinkle with ¼ cup sugar. Top with half the bread. Cover with remaining apples and sprinkle again with ¼ cup sugar. Combine orange and lemon juices; sprinkle over layers. Spread marmalade on remaining bread pieces. Arrange over apples. Bake 45 minutes. Remove from oven and reduce oven temperature to 300°. Beat egg whites until frothy. Gradually beat in ⅓ cup sugar, beating until stiff peaks are formed. Spoon egg white mixture onto baked apples, forming 6 mounds. Bake 15 minutes, or until meringue is lightly browned. Serve warm.

Apple Crumb

4 servings

4 cups sliced apples
½ cup butter

½ cup all-purpose flour
½ cup sugar

Preheat oven to 450°. Grease a 1-quart baking dish. Place apples in dish. Pour in ¼ cup hot water. Combine butter, flour, and sugar, stirring until mixture is crumbly. Spread over apples. Bake 10 minutes. Reduce heat to 350° and continue baking 30 minutes, or until apples are cooked. Serve with heavy cream.

Variation: For a change in flavor, add ¼ teaspoon mace or ½ teaspoon cinnamon to the crumb mixture. Or sprinkle ½ cup chopped walnuts or butternuts over the apples before the crumbs are added.

Nutty Apples

6 servings

6 cooking apples, peeled and cored
2 tablespoons sugar
⅛ teaspoon salt
¼ teaspoon ground cinnamon

½ cup firmly packed brown sugar
½ cup butter
1 cup finely chopped nuts

Preheat oven to 450°. Generously grease an oblong cake pan. Cut each apple into 8 pieces and place in parallel rows in cake pan. Combine sugar, salt, and cinnamon and sprinkle over apples. Cream together brown sugar and butter until light and fluffy. Add nuts. Spread mixture over and between apples, then pat to make a smooth surface. Bake 30 minutes, or until apples are tender. Serve warm with heavy cream.

Rhubarb Tapioca

4 to 6 servings

¾ cup pearl tapioca
½ teaspoon salt
3 cups chopped rhubarb

1 cup sugar
⅛ teaspoon ground nutmeg

Cover tapioca generously with cold water in a deep bowl and let stand several hours, or overnight; tapioca should absorb all the water. Place in the top part of a double boiler. Add 2½ cups boiling water and the salt. Cook over medium heat, stirring, until mixture comes to a boil. Place over boiling water and cook until tapioca is transparent. Preheat oven to 350°. Grease a baking dish or casserole and add rhubarb. Cover with sugar and sprinkle with nutmeg. Pour tapioca over top of rhubarb. Bake 20 to 30 minutes, or until rhubarb is soft. Serve warm or cold with cream or lemon sauce, if desired.

Rhubarb Delight

4 to 6 servings

2¼ cups fine dry bread crumbs
1½ cups firmly packed light brown
  sugar
2 tablespoons granulated white sugar
¼ teaspoon salt
¼ teaspoon ground nutmeg

½ teaspoon ground cinnamon
½ cup melted butter
6 cups chopped rhubarb
2 tablespoons lemon juice
1 tablespoon grated lemon peel

Preheat oven to 350°. Grease a 1½-quart baking dish. Mix bread crumbs, brown sugar, white sugar, salt, nutmeg, and cinnamon. Blend in butter. Mix rhubarb with lemon juice and lemon peel. Place alternate layers of crumb mixture and rhubarb in baking dish, ending with crumb mixture. Press top layer down. Bake 35 minutes, or until rhubarb is tender. Serve hot or cold.

Blueberry Crisp

6 servings

2½ cups fresh blueberries
1 tablespoon lemon juice
¾ cup firmly packed brown sugar
½ cup unsifted all-purpose flour

¼ teaspoon salt
¼ teaspoon ground nutmeg
¼ cup butter
Vanilla ice cream

Preheat oven to 400°. Butter the sides and bottom of a 2-quart baking dish. Pick over and wash blueberries. Drain thoroughly. Spread in baking dish. Sprinkle with lemon juice. Combine brown sugar, flour, salt, and nutmeg. With a pastry blender or two knives, cut in butter until mixture is crumbly. Sprinkle evenly over top of blueberries. Bake 15 to 20 minutes, or until hot and bubbling. Serve warm with vanilla ice cream.

Blueberry Betty

Blueberries were one of the many foods that the original Americans taught the settlers to use and appreciate. The first mention of blueberries occurred in 1616, when Samuel de Champlain found the Indians near Lake Huron gathering the berries for their winter store. "After drying the berries in the sun," Champlain relates in his journal, "the Indians beat them into a powder and add this powder to parched meal to make a dish called Sautauthig." Other Indians cured venison by pounding blueberries into the flesh and then smoke-drying the meat. The settlers saw the possibilities for making sweets, of which they were so fond, from the pretty and delicious berries.

4 cups fresh blueberries
3 tablespoons melted butter
2 cups fresh bread crumbs
½ cup firmly packed brown sugar

1 teaspoon ground cinnamon
1 tablespoon grated lemon peel
2 tablespoons lemon juice

Preheat oven to 375°. Grease a 1½-quart baking dish well. Rinse blueberries and let drain well in a colander. Toss melted butter with bread crumbs. Combine brown sugar, cinnamon, and lemon peel. Set aside. Sprinkle one-third of the crumbs in bottom of baking dish. Cover with half the drained blueberries. Sprinkle with half the sugar mixture. Repeat layers, ending with a layer of crumbs. Combine lemon juice with ¼ cup hot water and spoon evenly over top of layers. Bake 30 minutes. Serve warm with plain or whipped cream or ice cream, if desired.

Steamed Blueberry Pudding

1½ cups fresh blueberries
2½ cups sifted all-purpose flour
¼ cup butter, softened
¾ cup sugar
1 egg, well beaten

½ teaspoon vanilla extract
½ teaspoon lemon extract
½ teaspoon baking soda
1 cup buttermilk

Generously grease a 1-quart pudding mold, including the inside of the cover. (If you do not have a mold, use a coffee can and cover the top with heavy-duty aluminum foil.) Pick over blueberries and wash well; dry on absorbent paper. When dry, toss lightly with about 1 tablespoon of the flour. Cream butter and sugar together until light and fluffy. Beat in egg. Stir in vanilla and lemon extracts. Combine baking soda with buttermilk, stirring well. Add flour and buttermilk alternately to creamed butter, beginning and ending with flour; blend thoroughly. Fold in floured blueberries. Turn into mold and smooth out top. Cover securely with lid, or tie foil over top of coffee can. Place on a rack in a large pot. Pour in sufficient boiling water to come to within 1 inch of the top of the mold. Cover pot tightly, bring to a boil, reduce heat, and steam 3 hours, adding more boiling water during cooking period as needed. Lift mold carefully from the pot. Remove lid and run a knife around edge of pudding. Turn out on a serving platter and serve warm with hard sauce or whipped cream flavored with brandy.

Baked Pears

Preheat oven to 300°. Fill an earthen bean pot with Sheldon or Seckel pears, left whole and unpeeled but washed and clean. For each quart of fruit combine ½ cup brown sugar, ½ cup maple sugar, ½ cup hot water, and ½ teaspoon ginger and pour over fruit. Bake 1½ hours, or until tender, replacing water as needed in order to keep pears from burning.

Filled Pears
12 servings

12 medium-size pears
1 cup sugar
½ cup chopped dates
½ cup chopped nuts
½ cup seedless raisins

Peel and core pears. Place in a large saucepan with 1 cup water. Cover and simmer just until tender, adding more water if necessary during cooking time so that pears do not dry out and scorch. Carefully remove pears and place on a serving dish. Stir sugar into liquid remaining in saucepan and cook to a thick syrup, adding more water if necessary. Roll pears in syrup, draining off excess syrup, and return to serving dish. Add dates, nuts, and raisins to remaining syrup. Stir well. Fill cavities of pears with mixture. Cool before serving.

Concord Grape Tart
8 servings

Unsifted all-purpose flour
2 tablespoons sugar
3 egg yolks, divided
6 tablespoons butter,
  melted and cooled
2 cups grape preserve
1 tablespoon lemon juice
1 teaspoon grated lemon peel
1 cup dairy sour cream

Preheat oven to 350°. Mix 1 cup flour with the sugar. Stir in 1 egg yolk until mixture is thoroughly blended. Add butter and mix until a soft dough forms. Divide dough in half. Press one half into bottom of an 8-inch spring-form pan. Shape remaining half into a 3½-inch roll. Cut into 14 equal slices. Place slices around side walls of pan, pressing them firmly together and against sides, to form a tart shell with a scalloped edge. Bake 10 minutes; let cool. Combine preserve and 3 tablespoons flour in a small saucepan. Heat, stirring until mixture is thickened. Stir in lemon juice and lemon peel. Pour into prepared tart shell. Raise oven temperature to 400°. Bake tart 10 minutes. Combine remaining 2 egg yolks with sour cream. Force through a pastry tube onto surface of tart, forming a lattice pattern on top. Bake 15 to 20 minutes, or until topping is golden. Cool to room temperature before serving.

Concord Grape Trifle

4 egg yolks
Sugar
2 teaspoons vanilla extract
1 cup milk
1 cup light cream

2 sponge cake layers
½ cup sherry, divided
½ cup concord grape jam
⅓ cup shelled almonds, divided
1 cup heavy cream

In the top of a double boiler, beat egg yolks with ½ cup sugar until well blended. Add vanilla; stir in milk and light cream. Place over boiling water and cook, stirring, until custard is thick enough to coat a spoon, about 15 minutes. Chill several hours. Place 1 layer of sponge cake in a large crystal bowl. Pour half the sherry over the cake; spread with ½ cup jam. Stud cake layer with half the almonds. Repeat with remaining layer. Refrigerate until serving time. Combine heavy cream and remaining 1 tablespoon sugar. Beat until stiff. Just before serving, pour custard over cake layers. Top with whipped cream. Garnish with frosted grapes and additional almonds, if desired.

Note: *To frost grapes for the garnish, break the grapes into small bunches; dip each bunch into slightly beaten egg white, then into sugar. Dry on racks.*

Sweet Potato Pone

6 to 8 servings

This is one of the many imaginative uses that the colonists found for sweet potatoes. In many places in the South, to this day, if you ask for potatoes, you will be served sweet potatoes; if you want white potatoes, you must ask for Irish potatoes. Sweet potato dishes from the South are simple but distinctive, subtly seasoned and a welcome change of pace both in the main part of the meal and at dessert time. Versatile sweet potatoes can be made into croquettes, puddings, and pies, or combined with apples in a casserole.

6 cups grated raw sweet potatoes
½ cup butter, cut in pieces
1 cup milk
¼ cup molasses
2 tablespoons lemon juice
1 cup firmly packed brown sugar

1 tablespoon grated lemon peel
1 teaspoon ground ginger
½ teaspoon ground cinnamon
⅛ teaspoon ground nutmeg
Sweetened whipped cream

Preheat oven to 350°. Grease a shallow 1½-quart baking dish. In a large bowl blend potatoes, butter, milk, molasses, and lemon juice. In a small bowl combine brown sugar, lemon peel, ginger, cinnamon, and nutmeg. Add to potato mixture and blend well. Turn into baking dish. Bake 1 hour. Serve warm with whipped cream.

Plymouth Rock Pudding

6 servings

4 large raw sweet potatoes
2 eggs
1 cup molasses

½ cup milk
½ cup butter, melted
½ teaspoon salt

Preheat oven to 350°. Grease a 2-quart casserole or baking dish. Pare and grate sweet potatoes. Beat eggs well; add molasses, milk, melted butter, and salt. Stir in grated sweet potatoes. Turn into casserole. Bake about 2 hours, or until pudding is very dark and caramel-colored. Serve warm, with lemon sauce, if desired.

Note: *Don't make the mistake of grating the potatoes in advance. Prepare them just before you are ready to use them, or they will turn dark and make an unsightly pudding.*

Sweet Potato Pudding

4 to 6 servings

3 eggs, separated
2 cups cooked, mashed sweet
  potatoes
¼ teaspoon ground nutmeg
¼ teaspoon ground cloves
½ teaspoon ground cinnamon

½ cup sugar
½ cup butter, melted
2 tablespoons red wine
2 tablespoons brandy
½ cup milk
Sugar and cinnamon (optional)

Preheat oven to 350°. Grease a 2-quart casserole. Beat egg yolks lightly. Stir in sweet potatoes to make a smooth mixture. Stir in spices, sugar, butter, wine, brandy, and milk and beat thoroughly. Beat egg whites until stiff but not dry. Fold into sweet potato mixture. Heap mixture in casserole. Sprinkle lightly with sugar and cinnamon, if desired. Bake about 1 hour, or until lightly browned on top.

Note: *Although today we would call this a dessert pudding, it was originally served with chicken, ham, or pork for dinner.*

Today's Indian Pudding

8 servings

2 cups corn-bread crumbs
4 cups milk
2 eggs, lightly beaten
⅔ cup maple syrup

½ teaspoon ground cinnamon
¼ teaspoon ground ginger
½ teaspoon salt
1 tablespoon melted butter

Preheat oven to 350°. Grease a 2-quart casserole. Combine corn-bread crumbs and milk and let stand 10 minutes. Beat in eggs, syrup, spices, and salt. Stir in butter. Pour into casserole. Bake 1½ hours. After the first 30 minutes of baking, slide a spoon under top crust and stir pudding gently without stirring crust into pudding. Serve warm or cold with heavy cream, whipped cream, or ice cream.

Indian Pudding

8 *servings*

There are at least as many versions of Indian Pudding as there were original colonies, and probably more. In some places the pudding was sweetened with molasses, in some with maple sugar. Sometimes it was precooked and then baked in the dutch oven along with breads and pies.

5 cups milk, divided
⅔ cup dark molasses
⅓ cup sugar
½ cup yellow cornmeal

¾ teaspoon ground cinnamon
¾ teaspoon ground nutmeg
1 teaspoon salt
¼ cup butter

Preheat oven to 300°. Grease a 1½-quart baking dish. Heat 4 cups milk. Stir in molasses, sugar, cornmeal, cinnamon, nutmeg, salt, and butter. Cook, stirring constantly, until mixture thickens. Pour into baking dish. Pour remaining cup of cold milk carefully over top. Do not stir. Bake 3 hours without stirring. Serve warm with cream, ice cream, or hard sauce.

Quick Indian Pudding

8 *servings*

5 cups milk, divided
5 tablespoons yellow cornmeal
2 tablespoons butter
1 cup dark molasses

1 teaspoon salt
¾ teaspoon ground cinnamon
½ teaspoon ground ginger
2 eggs, lightly beaten

Preheat oven to 350°. Grease a 1½-quart baking dish. Put 4 cups milk in the top part of a double boiler. Bring just to a boil over direct heat. Slowly add cornmeal, stirring constantly. Place over boiling water and cook 15 minutes, stirring occasionally. Stir in butter, molasses, salt, cinnamon, and ginger. Beat eggs into mixture. Turn into a baking dish. Pour remaining cup of cold milk over top of mixture. Do not stir. Bake 1 hour. Serve warm with ice cream or heavy cream.

Company Indian Pudding

6 *servings*

1 quart milk
¼ cup white cornmeal
3 eggs
¼ cup sugar

¾ teaspoon salt
½ teaspoon ground ginger
1 tablespoon light molasses
1 tablespoon butter

Preheat oven to 350°. Grease a 1½-quart baking dish. Heat milk in top part of double boiler over low heat. Add cornmeal gradually, stirring until smooth. Place over boiling water and cook about 15 minutes, or until thickened, stirring occasionally. Beat together eggs, sugar, salt, ginger, and molasses. Stir butter into cornmeal mixture until it is melted. Pour cornmeal mixture gradually into beaten egg mixture, stirring constantly. Pour into baking dish. Bake 50 to 60 minutes, or until set. Serve hot with heavy cream or ice cream.

An Indian Pudding boiled.

One quart of milk, and three half-pints· of Indian meal, and a gill of molaſſes, then put it in a cloth, and let it boil seven, or eight hours. The water boiling when it is put in. Water may be used instead of milk in case you have none.

To make a baked Indian Pudding

Rather than duplicating this pudding, which is rather bland, try one of the recipes given in this section for an Indian Pudding, which will appeal more to present-day tastes.

To make ice cream at home

1. Prepare ice cream mix and chill thoroughly.
2. Set out rock salt and measuring cups.
3. Use packaged crushed ice to give the ice cream finer texture.
4. Pour chilled mix into freezer can, filling it no more than ⅔ full to leave room for expansion. Insert dasher and put cover on tightly.
5. Make layers of rock salt and ice around container until tub is tightly packed. Use 1 cup of rock salt to 2 quarts of crushed ice. (If too much rock salt is used, the ice cream will freeze too rapidly and will have a coarse texture, or a crust may freeze around the edge of the can, which will interfere with rotation.)
6. Turn hand crank until turning becomes labored.
7. Carefully remove the cover, brushing away salt and ice. Lift out dasher and scrape the ice cream back into the can. Cork or plug the cover. Place waxed paper across the top of the can, then replace the cover.
8. Pour off brine and pack container with more salt and crushed ice in the same proportion.
9. Cover with towel, rug, or newspapers to insulate. Let stand 1 hour, or until hardened.

Vanilla Custard Ice Cream   *1½ quarts*

Ice cream was much prized as an elegant dessert in the 1700s. When George Washington returned to Mount Vernon after the Revolution, one of his early acquisitions was an ice cream freezer. The story goes that Thomas Jefferson, perhaps the first American gourmet, later amazed his guests at a White House dinner by serving vanilla ice cream shaped in small balls and baked in pastry—an early version of Baked Alaska.

¾ cup sugar	1 quart light cream, divided
2 tablespoons all-purpose flour	2 eggs, lightly beaten
¼ teaspoon salt	1½ tablespoons vanilla extract

In a heavy 2-quart saucepan combine sugar, flour, and salt. Gradually add 2 cups of the cream and stir well. Cook over medium heat, stirring constantly, until mixture is thickened and comes to a boil. Cook 2 more minutes, stirring constantly. Add a small amount of the hot mixture to the beaten eggs, stirring well. Add to mixture in pan. Cook, stirring constantly, 1 minute. Remove from heat and stir in remaining 2 cups cream and vanilla. Chill thoroughly. Freeze according to preceding directions, or follow those accompanying ice cream freezer.

Maple Cup Custard   *6 to 8 servings*

4 eggs, lightly beaten	Pinch of salt
3 cups milk	¼ teaspoon vanilla extract
¾ cup maple syrup	

Preheat oven to 350°. Beat together eggs, milk, maple syrup, salt, and vanilla. Pour into 6 to 8 custard cups. Set cups in a pan of hot water. Bake about 45 minutes, or until a knife inserted in center of custard comes out clean. Remove from hot water and cool before serving.

Southern Peanut Pie   *1 9-inch pie*

2 eggs	1 teaspoon vanilla extract
1 cup dark corn syrup	1 cup dry roasted peanuts
1 cup sugar	1 9-inch pastry shell
¼ teaspoon salt	2 tablespoons butter

Preheat oven to 350°. Beat eggs until foamy. Beat in syrup, sugar, salt, and vanilla. Stir in peanuts. Pour mixture into unbaked pastry shell. Dot top with butter. Bake 45 to 50 minutes, or until filling is set. Cool before serving.

Wild Blackberry Deep-Dish Pie

6 servings

5 cups wild blackberries
2 tablespoons butter
2 cups sugar, divided

4 tablespoons cornstarch
Pastry for a 1-crust 9-inch
pie

Preheat oven to 400°. Grease a 9-inch square baking dish. Spread 4 cups of the washed and drained blackberries in dish. Dot with butter and sprinkle with ½ cup sugar. Cook 1 cup wild blackberries with 1½ cups sugar just until they begin to soften. Combine cornstarch and ⅓ cup cold water. Stir into blackberries in saucepan and cook, stirring constantly, until clear and thickened. Pour cooked berries over top of blackberries in baking dish. Roll out pastry to ¼-inch thickness. Cut into strips and weave in a lattice pattern over top of berries. Crimp and seal pastry around edge of dish. Bake 15 minutes. Reduce heat to 350° and continue baking 25 to 30 minutes, or until pastry is lightly browned and berries are cooked. Serve slightly warm with whipped cream or ice cream.

Rhubarb Pie

1 9-inch pie

Pastry for a 2-crust 9-inch pie
1¼ cups firmly packed light brown
  sugar

2 tablespoons all-purpose flour
3½ to 4 cups sliced raw rhubarb
1 lemon

Preheat oven to 375°. Line a 9-inch pie plate with half the pastry. Combine sugar and flour and sprinkle a third of the mixture over pastry in pie plate. Cover with a layer of rhubarb. Peel lemon with a knife, removing all of white membrane. Cut in very thin slices. Place a few lemon slices on top of rhubarb. Continue layers until all ingredients are used. Make strips from remaining pastry and cover top of pie with a lattice crust. Bake 50 to 60 minutes, or until rhubarb is cooked and crust is lightly browned.

Huldah's Buttermilk Pie

1 9-inch pie

In colonial days, and for a long time thereafter, buttermilk was not the pre-pared beverage we find in our supermarket dairy cases today, but the by-product of butter churning. Chilled in a convenient swift-running stream, it was valued as a thirst quencher and was used interchangeably with sour milk in cooking.

3 eggs, separated
2 cups buttermilk
1 cup sugar
¼ teaspoon salt

3 tablespoons all-purpose flour
4 teaspoons melted butter
1 teaspoon vanilla extract
1 9-inch pastry shell

Preheat oven to 450°. Beat egg yolks thoroughly. Beat in buttermilk. Combine sugar, salt, and flour. Stir into egg mixture and blend well. Stir in butter and vanilla. Beat egg whites until they stand in stiff peaks. Fold into buttermilk mixture. Pour into unbaked pastry shell. Bake 10 minutes. Reduce heat to 350° and bake 30 to 35 minutes, or until pie is set. The pie will get very brown on top.

Plymouth Cranberry Pie

1 9-inch pie

3 to 4 cups cranberries
1 cup sugar
1 egg, lightly beaten

½ teaspoon almond extract
Pastry for a 2-crust 9-inch pie

Preheat oven to 400°. Wash and pick over cranberries; drain thoroughly. Chop cranberries and mix with sugar. Mix egg and almond extract and combine with cranberries. Line a 9-inch pie plate with half the pastry. Add cranberry mixture. Cover with strips of pastry arranged in a lattice, and seal edges. Bake 10 minutes. Reduce heat to 350° and continue baking about 35 minutes, or until cranberries are soft and pastry is browned.

Dry-Type Shoofly Pie

8 servings

1¼ cups sifted all-purpose flour
⅔ cup firmly packed brown sugar
½ teaspoon ground cinnamon
¼ teaspoon ground nutmeg
¼ teaspoon ground ginger
¼ teaspoon ground cloves

½ teaspoon salt
3 tablespoons butter
1 egg yolk, well beaten
⅔ cup light molasses
1½ teaspoons baking soda
1 9-inch pastry shell

Preheat oven to 450°. Sift together flour, sugar, spices, and salt. Cut in butter with a pastry blender or two knives until mixture resembles corn-meal. In a small bowl, combine egg yolk and molasses. Dissolve baking soda in 1 cup boiling water. Stir into molasses mixture. Fill pastry shell with alternate layers of flour mixture and molasses mixture, starting and ending with a layer of flour. Bake 10 minutes. Reduce heat to 350° and bake 15 to 20 minutes, or until pie is set. Remove to wire rack to cool.

Old-Fashioned Apple Pie

1 9-inch pie

Early pie crusts were made with meat drippings or lard and would perhaps be tough by today's standards. But the settlers loved pies and sometimes ate them for breakfast. In those days pies were not made one or two at a time; as many as fifty might be made in the winter, when the baked pies could be frozen. When a pie was wanted, it was brought indoors and set in front of the fire to thaw and warm.

6 to 8 large tart apples, peeled, cored, and quartered	2 teaspoons all-purpose flour
	¼ teaspoon ground nutmeg
Pastry for a 2-crust 9-inch pie	½ teaspoon ground cinnamon
1 cup sugar	2 tablespoons butter

Preheat oven to 425°. Cut apples in thin slices. Line a 9-inch pie pan with a little over half the pastry. Mix sugar, flour, and spices; rub a little sugar mixture into pastry. Arrange apple slices in pan. Top with remaining sugar mixture. Dot with butter. Cover with top crust and seal edges. Cut slits in top crust. Bake 40 to 45 minutes, or until apples are tender and crust is nicely browned.

Sour Cream Pumpkin Pie

1 9-inch pie

1 cup sifted all-purpose flour	1 can (1 pound) solid-pack pumpkin
Salt	
3 tablespoons butter	¾ cup firmly packed light brown sugar
2 tablespoons lard	
½ cup finely chopped pecans	2 teaspoons ground cinnamon
3 tablespoons milk	1 teaspoon ground nutmeg
1½ cups dairy sour cream	½ teaspoon ground cloves
3 eggs, separated	2 tablespoons sugar

Preheat oven to 375°. Sift together flour and ¼ teaspoon salt. Cut in butter and lard with a pastry blender or two knives until mixture resembles small peas. Add pecans. Sprinkle on milk, one tablespoon at a time, mixing lightly with a fork. Gather up dough with fingers and shape into a ball. On a lightly floured board, roll out dough into a 10-inch circle ⅛ inch thick. Ease dough into a 9-inch pie plate. Build up edge on rim of pie plate and flute. In a 2-quart saucepan stir sour cream, egg yolks, pumpkin, brown sugar, cinnamon, nutmeg, cloves, and ½ teaspoon salt. Cook over low heat, stirring occasionally, 15 minutes, or until mixture thickens. Beat egg whites until foamy; gradually add sugar and continue beating until stiff peaks form. Gradually fold pumpkin mixture into beaten egg whites. Mound mixture into pie shell. Bake 20 to 30 minutes, or until a knife inserted near center comes out clean. Cool on wire rack. Garnish with sweetened whipped cream, if desired.

Apple Pye.

Stew and ſtrain the apples, to every three pints, grate the peal of a freſh lemon, add cinnamon, mace, roſewater and ſugar to your taſte ; and bake in paſte No. 3.

Every ſpecies of fruit ſuch as peas, raſpberries, blackberries may be only ſweetened, without ſpices ; and bake in paſte No. 3.

Apple Pie   *1 9-inch pie*

3 pounds cooking apples   *¼ teaspoon ground mace*
½ cup sugar   *1 teaspoon rose water*
Grated peel of 1 lemon   *Pastry for a 1-crust 9-inch pie*
¼ teaspoon ground cinnamon

Preheat oven to 450°. Peel, core, and cut apples into slices about ½ inch thick. Place in a saucepan with sugar. Add just enough water to cover bottom of saucepan. Cover and simmer gently, just until apples begin to break apart. Drain off excess liquid. Combine gently with lemon peel, cinnamon, mace, and rose water. Taste and add more sugar if needed. Line a 9-inch pie pan with half the pastry. Turn apples into pastry. Top with remaining pastry. Crimp edges and cut a few slashes in top crust of pie. Bake 10 minutes. Reduce heat to 375° and continue baking 25 minutes, or until crust is golden brown.

Note: *Paste No. 3 was made from 1 pound (4 cups) flour and ¾ pound (1½ cups) butter, rubbed together with the fingers to make it crumbly. Then just enough water was added to make the dough stick together. The dough was rolled out for the pie.*

Grandmother Pratt's Strawberry Crumb Pie   *1 9-inch pie*

3 pints fresh strawberries,
  cleaned and halved
¾ cup sugar
¼ cup cornstarch
1⅓ cups sifted all-purpose flour

½ teaspoon salt
⅓ cup shortening
¼ cup firmly packed light brown sugar
½ teaspoon ground cinnamon
Cream

Preheat oven to 400°. Combine strawberries with sugar and cornstarch. Set aside. Combine flour and salt in a bowl. Cut in shortening with a pastry blender or two knives until mixture is coarse. Set aside ⅔ cup of the mixture. Sprinkle 2 to 3 tablespoons water over remainder and toss with a fork until mixed and mixture sticks together. Press with hands into a ball. Roll out on a lightly floured board into a circle ½ inch larger than an inverted 9-inch pie plate. Fit dough carefully into plate. Turn under edges to make a double thickness around edge and flute so that edge is high. Fill with strawberry mixture. Combine reserved flour mixture, brown sugar, and cinnamon and blend well. Sprinkle over strawberries. Place pie in oven on a sheet of aluminum foil. Bake 45 minutes, or until crust is browned. Serve warm or cold, with cream.

Lobster Cake   *8 to 10 servings*

3 cups sifted all-purpose flour
¾ teaspoon cream of tartar
½ teaspoon baking soda
¼ teaspoon salt
1 cup butter
2 cups sugar
4 eggs, beaten

1 cup milk
½ cup light molasses
½ teaspoon ground cloves
¼ teaspoon ground nutmeg
½ cup chopped seedless raisins
½ cup chopped citron

Grease a 15- x 9- x 2-inch loaf pan. Preheat oven to 350°. Sift together flour, cream of tartar, baking soda, and salt three times. Cream together butter and sugar until light and fluffy. Beat in eggs until well blended. Add flour mixture alternately with milk, beginning and ending with flour. Beat until smooth. Divide mixture in half. To one part add molasses, cloves, and nutmeg. To the other part add raisins and citron. Drop by tablespoonfuls into loaf pan, alternating light and dark mixtures. Bake 1 hour, or until cake springs back in center when lightly touched with the fingers. Remove cake and cool on rack. Cake can be frosted or not, as desired.

Note: *No one seems to know why this was called Lobster Cake. We might guess that because of the two batters and the raisins and citron, the cake, when baked, looks somewhat like the speckled pattern of the shell of an uncooked lobster.*

Cocoa Cake

1 2-layer cake

1 cup dairy sour cream
2 eggs
1 teaspoon vanilla extract
1½ cups sifted cake flour

1 teaspoon baking soda
½ teaspoon salt
2½ tablespoons cocoa
1 cup sugar

Preheat oven to 375°. Grease and flour two 9-inch layer cake pans. Beat together thoroughly the sour cream and eggs. Beat in vanilla. Sift together flour, baking soda, salt, cocoa, and sugar. Add dry ingredients to sour cream mixture and beat well. Turn batter into prepared cake pans. Bake 25 to 30 minutes, or until a cake tester inserted in the center comes out clean. Cool on wire racks 5 minutes. Remove from pans and cool. Serve dusted with confectioners sugar or frosted, as desired.

Williamsburg Orange Cake

8 servings

½ cup butter
1 cup sugar
2 eggs
1 teaspoon vanilla extract
1⅔ cups unsifted all-purpose flour
1 teaspoon baking soda

½ teaspoon salt
1 cup sour milk or buttermilk
1 cup chopped dark seedless raisins
½ cup coarsely chopped walnuts
1 tablespoon grated orange peel
Orange Wine Icing

Preheat oven to 350°. Grease and flour an 8-inch square baking pan. Cream together butter and sugar until light and fluffy. Beat in eggs and vanilla. In a small bowl blend flour, baking soda, and salt. Add to butter mixture alternately with sour milk, beginning and ending with flour mixture. Blend well after each addition. Stir in raisins, walnuts, and orange peel. Pour mixture into prepared pan. Bake 45 to 50 minutes, or until cake tester comes out clean when inserted in center of cake. Cool in pan on wire rack for 10 minutes. Remove from pan and cool thoroughly on wire rack. When cool, frost with Orange Wine Icing.

Orange Wine Icing

2 cups unsifted confectioners sugar
⅓ cup softened butter

1 tablespoon grated orange peel
2 tablespoons cream sherry

Mix together sugar, butter, and orange peel until well blended. Add sherry and beat until smooth. Use to frost Williamsburg Orange Cake.

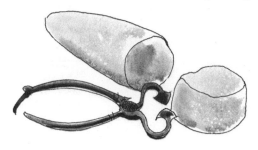

Old South Pound Cake

1 10-inch ring cake

1½ cups butter
1 pound confectioners sugar
6 eggs

2 teaspoons vanilla extract
2½ cups sifted all-purpose flour
½ teaspoon salt

Preheat oven to 325°. Grease a 10-inch bundt or tube pan well. Cream butter until light. Gradually beat in confectioners sugar until light and fluffy. Add eggs, one at a time, beating well after each addition. Stir in vanilla. Gradually add flour and salt, folding into creamed mixture by hand. Blend well. Pour batter into pan. Cut through batter with a knife several times to remove air bubbles. Bake 1 hour, or until a cake tester inserted in cake comes out clean. Cool in pan on a rack 10 minutes. Turn cake out of pan and cool thoroughly. Dust with confectioners sugar before serving, if desired.

Pork Cake

2 loaf cakes

The fatback in this recipe may seem strange to today's cooks, but we should remember that whatever was at hand was turned to use in colonial cookery. Colonial women often used vegetables, meat, and herbs in their desserts; for example, they made sweet fritters from vegetables and served them with a wine sauce. Even in the present day, true mincemeat for pies is still made with minced meat and suet is the shortening in various steamed spice-and-fruit puddings.

½ pound fat salt pork (called
   fatback, with no lean)
4 cups sifted all-purpose
   flour
1 teaspoon baking soda
Pinch of salt
1 teaspoon ground cinnamon
1 teaspoon ground cloves

1 teaspoon ground allspice
1 teaspoon ground nutmeg
1 cup seedless raisins,
   chopped
2 eggs, beaten
1 cup sugar
1 cup molasses

Put salt pork through food chopper, using finest blade. Place in a bowl; cover with 1 cup of boiling water and let stand 15 minutes. Grease generously and flour two 9- x 5- x 3-inch loaf pans; set aside. Preheat oven to 325°. Sift together flour, baking soda, salt, cinnamon, cloves, allspice, and nutmeg. Stir in raisins until well blended. Combine eggs, sugar, molasses, and salt pork mixture. Pour into flour mixture and stir just enough to blend; do not overbeat. Pour mixture into prepared pans. Bake 50 to 60 minutes, or until a toothpick inserted in center comes out clean. Let stand in pans 5 minutes. Turn out on cooling rack and cool thoroughly.

Note: *More raisins may be used if desired; nuts may also be added or substituted for the raisins. Traditionally, four or more loaves were made at one time because this cake keeps well—in fact, if carefully wrapped it will keep for several weeks. Or you may wrap it well in moisture-proof material and freeze.*

Almond Cheese-cakes.

Take halfe a Pound of Jordan Almonds, Beat them very well with Orange flower water, & a little Cream: then put to them halfe a pound of Sugar & four Eggs well beaten & a quarter of a pound of Butter melted. Stirr it well together. Make Puffe past for the Crust, & put it into the Pans, & bake it a little, & then put in your Cheese-cake stuffe, & Bake them till it is enough.

Almond Cheesecakes

6 servings

¼ pound shelled almonds	6 tablespoons sugar
3 eggs	1 teaspoon rose water
¼ cup soft butter	6 unbaked 4-inch tart shells

Preheat oven to 375°. Put almonds in container of electric blender. Process at low speed until almonds are chopped very fine. Add eggs and beat until well mixed. Add butter, sugar, and rose water and blend thoroughly. Divide among tart shells. Bake 20 to 25 minutes, or until tarts are puffy and set.

Note: *As the original recipe produces an extremely sweet cake, the proportion of sugar originally called for has been reduced here. A standard pastry, rolled thin, works better than the puff paste recommended in the original; puff paste tends to become soggy when the filling is added. Rose water imparts a lovely, delicate flavor, but if it is unavailable, substitute an equal amount of lemon juice or ¼ teaspoon vanilla extract.*

Colonial Caraway Cake

12 to 14 *servings*

5 eggs, separated
¼ teaspoon salt
1½ cups sugar, divided
1 cup butter

2 teaspoons caraway seed
¾ teaspoon orange extract
1⅔ cups all-purpose
  flour

Preheat oven to 300°. Grease and lightly flour a 10-inch bundt or tube pan. Combine egg whites and salt in a large mixing bowl. Beat until mixture is frothy. Gradually beat in ½ cup sugar, beating until stiff peaks are formed. Set aside. Cream together butter and remaining 1 cup sugar until light and fluffy. Add egg yolks, one at a time, beating well after each addition. Beat in caraway seed and orange extract. Blend in flour just until smooth. Gently fold in half the meringue until mixture is fairly smooth. Gently fold in remaining meringue just until it is all incorporated. Turn mixture into prepared pan. Cut carefully through batter with spatula or knife three or four times. Bake 60 to 70 minutes, or until cake leaves the sides of the pan. Cool in pan 10 minutes. Remove from pan and cool on wire rack. Sprinkle with confectioners sugar before serving, if desired.

Hot Water Cake

9 *servings*

½ cup shortening
½ cup sugar
1 cup molasses
2½ cups sifted all-purpose
  flour

1½ teaspoons baking soda
½ teaspoon salt
½ teaspoon ground cinnamon
½ teaspoon ground allspice
½ teaspoon ground cloves

Preheat oven to 350°. Grease and flour a 9-inch square cake pan. Cream together shortening and sugar until light and fluffy. Stir in molasses. Sift together flour, baking soda, salt, cinnamon, allspice, and cloves. Stir into molasses mixture. Add 1 cup boiling water and mix well. Turn into prepared pan. Bake 30 to 35 minutes, or until a toothpick inserted in center comes out clean.

Black Cake

6 *servings*

2 cups sifted all-purpose flour
½ teaspoon baking soda
¼ teaspoon salt
½ teaspoon cream of tartar
½ teaspoon ground cloves
½ teaspoon ground nutmeg

½ cup seedless raisins, chopped
½ cup butter
¾ cup sugar
1 large egg
¼ cup molasses
½ cup milk

Preheat oven to 350°. Grease generously and flour an 8-inch square cake pan. Sift together flour, baking soda, salt, cream of tartar, cloves, and nutmeg. Remove ½ cup of flour mixture and toss lightly with raisins. Cream together butter and sugar until light and fluffy. Beat in egg. Combine molasses and milk. Add to butter mixture alternately with flour mixture, beginning and ending with flour. Stir in raisins. Turn into prepared pan. Bake 40 to 45 minutes, or until a toothpick inserted in center of cake comes out clean.

Sour Cream Spice Cake   6 servings

1 egg
½ pint (about) dairy sour cream
1 cup sugar
2 cups sifted all-purpose flour
¼ teaspoon salt
1 teaspoon baking soda

½ teaspoon ground cinnamon
½ teaspoon ground nutmeg
¼ teaspoon ground cloves
½ seedless raisins or chopped nuts

Preheat oven to 350°. Grease and flour an 8-inch square cake pan. Break egg into a 1-cup measuring cup. Fill cup with sour cream. Pour into a bowl, beat thoroughly with an egg beater. Add sugar and continue beating. Sift flour, salt, baking soda, and spices together. Add to sour cream mixture and mix just until well blended. Stir in raisins. Turn into prepared pan. Bake 40 to 45 minutes, or until a toothpick inserted in center of cake comes out clean.

Apple Dumplings   6 servings

2⅔ cups sifted all-purpose flour
1¼ teaspoons salt
1 cup shortening
⅓ cup firmly packed light brown sugar
⅓ cup finely chopped walnuts

¾ teaspoon ground cinnamon, divided
6 medium tart baking apples, peeled and cored
Cream or milk
2 tablespoons white granulated sugar

Preheat oven to 400°. Combine flour and salt in a bowl. Cut in shortening with a pastry blender or two knives until mixture is coarse. Sprinkle with 6½ tablespoons water, toss with a fork, and press into a ball. Combine brown sugar, walnuts, and ¼ teaspoon cinnamon; set aside. On a lightly floured board, roll out pastry to a 14- x 21-inch rectangle. Cut into six 7-inch squares. Place an apple on each square and fill cavity of each apple with nut mixture. Moisten edges of squares with cream. Bring opposite points of pastry up over apple and press together; repeat with remaining squares. Brush dumplings with cream. Blend 2 tablespoons granulated sugar with remaining ½ teaspoon cinnamon; sprinkle over top of pastry. Place dumplings on ungreased baking sheet and bake 30 to 35 minutes, or until brown.

Gingerbread with Raisins

9 servings

⅔ cup sugar
⅔ cup molasses
2 tablespoons butter
1 teaspoon baking soda
½ cup seedless raisins
½ cup chopped walnuts
1 egg, beaten

1½ cups sifted all-purpose
  flour
1 teaspoon ground cinnamon
1 teaspoon ground ginger
¼ teaspoon ground cloves
Whipped cream

Preheat oven to 350°. Thoroughly grease a 9-inch square pan. Combine sugar, molasses, and ⅔ cup boiling water in a mixing bowl. Stir in butter and baking soda. Let stand a few minutes to cool. Stir in raisins, nuts, and egg. Sift together flour and spices. Stir into mixture to make a smooth batter. Turn into pan. Bake 35 to 40 minutes, or until center of cake springs back when touched lightly with the fingers. Serve warm with whipped cream.

Note: *This gingerbread is delicious served hot with hot lemon sauce. To gild this old-fashioned treat still further, whip cream cheese with a little milk to soften it, and place a generous dab on the gingerbread before pouring on the lemon sauce.*

Shortnin' Bread

about 3 dozen

3 cups sifted all-purpose flour
½ cup sugar

1 cup butter
1 egg yolk

Preheat oven to 350°. Combine flour and sugar. Work in butter with fingertips until mixture is well blended. Add egg yolk and knead dough thoroughly until smooth. Divide dough into 4 equal parts. Pat each quarter into a square or circle ½ inch thick. Place on baking sheets and prick top with a fork. Bake 15 minutes. Reduce heat to 300°; bake 30 minutes. Cut each quarter into 8 pieces and return to oven long enough to brown edges.

Ginger Snaps

about 4 dozen

1 cup lard
1 cup molasses
1 teaspoon baking soda

2 teaspoons ground ginger
½ teaspoon salt
2½ cups (about) sifted all-purpose flour

In a saucepan, combine lard and molasses; bring to a boil and boil 2 minutes. Cool. Stir in soda, ginger, salt, and enough flour to make a stiff dough. Chill several hours or overnight. Preheat oven to 375°. Roll dough out a little at a time on a lightly floured board. Cut in desired shapes and place on lightly greased baking sheets. Bake about 8 minutes, or until lightly browned.

Sugar Cakes   *6 dozen*

6 egg yolks   *1 cup sugar*
4 egg whites   *1¼ cups sifted all-purpose flour*

Preheat oven to 325°. Put egg yolks and whites in the large bowl of
an electric mixer. Beat until thick and light in color. Add sugar slowly,
beating constantly, until mixture is thick and very pale in color. Turn
mixer to low setting and add flour by spoonfuls, beating constantly.
Scrape bottom and beaters with rubber scraper during mixing process.
Continue beating until flour is all folded in and batter is smooth. Drop
by spoonfuls onto a buttered baking sheet. Sprinkle sugar heavily over
tops of cookies. Bake 10 to 12 minutes, or until lightly browned around
edges. Take from oven and remove from baking sheets immediately.

Note: *These cookies are in the sponge cake family. They taste very good,
but they dry out and become crisp quite rapidly. They are at their best the
day they are made.*

Island Ginger Cookies   *2½ dozen*

½ cup butter
⅔ cup firmly packed light brown sugar
⅓ cup molasses

2 cups sifted all-purpose flour
1 teaspoon baking soda
1 teaspoon ground ginger

Preheat oven to 350°. Cream together butter and sugar until light and fluffy. Stir in molasses and ⅓ cup cold water. Sift together the flour, baking soda, and ginger. Add to creamed butter mixture and stir thoroughly. Drop by heaping teaspoonfuls onto well-greased baking sheets. Bake 11 or 12 minutes, or until lightly browned. Remove from baking sheets and cool on racks. Store in a tightly covered container.

Ginger Cookies   *6 dozen*

⅔ cup butter
½ cup sugar
1 egg
1 cup light molasses

1 tablespoon cider vinegar
4½ cups sifted all-purpose flour
1 tablespoon ground ginger
1 tablespoon baking soda

Cream together the butter and the sugar until mixture is light and fluffy. Beat n the egg and blend well. Stir in molasses, vinegar, and 2 tablespoons cold water. Sift together flour, ginger, and baking soda. Add gradually to butter mixture, stirring to make a stiff dough. Chill dough thoroughly, about 1 hour. Preheat oven to 350°. Roll dough out a little at a time on a lightly floured board; it can be rolled out thick or thin, depending on the kind of cookies desired. Cut into desired shapes and place on lightly greased baking sheets. Bake 12 to 14 minutes, or until lightly browned and set. Loosen immediately and place on racks to cool. Thick cookies can be sprinkled with a little confectioners sugar or can be spread with lemon-flavored confectioners sugar frosting.

Maple Ginger Snaps   *about 5 dozen*

Molasses was the favorite sweetener in colonial cookery, followed by maple sugar, which was free of charge (except for the labor of tapping the trees and boiling down the sap) to those who lived where maple trees grew. White sugar, too, was available—in blue-paper-wrapped loaves or cones from which chunks were cut and pounded to the desired fineness—but it was expensive.

2 cups soft maple sugar
1 cup butter
2 eggs, beaten
4 cups (about) sifted all-purpose flour

¼ teaspoon salt
1 tablespoon ground ginger
1 teaspoon baking soda
1 cup dairy sour cream

Cream together sugar and butter until light and fluffy. Beat in the eggs. Sift together flour, salt, and ginger. Add baking soda to sour cream. Add flour mixture alternately with the cream to sugar mixture, blending well after each addition. Use enough flour to make a stiff dough. Chill 1 hour. Preheat oven to 375°. Roll dough out thin on a lightly floured board. Cut into desired shapes with a floured cutter. Place on lightly greased baking sheets and bake about 8 minutes, or until lightly browned.

Molasses Applesauce Cookies
about 7½ dozen

2 cups sifted all-purpose flour
1 teaspoon baking soda
1 teaspoon salt
2 teaspoons ground cinnamon
½ teaspoon ground cloves
½ cup shortening

½ cup sugar
½ cup molasses
1 egg
1 cup applesauce
½ cup chopped raisins
½ cup chopped nuts

Preheat oven to 350°. Sift together flour, baking soda, salt, cinnamon, and cloves. Cream together shortening, sugar, and molasses. Beat in egg. Blend in dry ingredients and applesauce. Stir in raisins and nuts. Drop by teaspoonfuls onto lightly greased baking sheets. Bake 10 to 12 minutes, or until lightly browned. Remove from sheets and cool on wire racks.

Butter Thins
4½ to 5 dozen

1 cup soft butter
1 cup sugar
3 egg yolks

2½ cups sifted all-purpose flour
1 teaspoon vanilla

Preheat oven to 350° F. Cream together butter and sugar until light and fluffy. Add egg yolks and beat thoroughly. Add flour and stir in until mixture is well blended. Add vanilla. Chill. Roll dough out on a lightly floured board to ⅛-inch thickness. Cut with a 2½-inch cookie cutter. Place on lightly oiled baking sheet and bake 10 to 12 minutes or until lightly browned. Cool on wire racks.

Rum Drops
2½ to 3 dozen

1 cup light brown sugar, firmly packed
½ cup shortening
1 egg
1½ cups sifted all-purpose flour
½ teaspoon baking soda

½ teaspoon salt
1 teaspoon ground nutmeg
1 cup finely chopped unpeeled apples
Rum

Preheat oven to 375° F. Cream together sugar and shortening until light and fluffy. Beat in egg. Sift together flour, soda, salt, and nutmeg. Add to creamed mixture and stir well. Stir in apples. Drop by teaspoonfuls onto oiled baking sheets. Bake 12 to 15 minutes. Remove from oven and sprinkle 4 to 5 drops of rum on top of each cookie. Remove from baking sheet and cool on wire racks.

Tasty Bacon Cookies

3½ dozen

½ cup bacon drippings
¾ cup molasses
2 tablespoons sugar
2 cups sifted all-purpose flour
¾ teaspoon salt

1 teaspoon baking soda
1 teaspoon ground cinnamon
¾ teaspoon ground ginger
¼ teaspoon ground cloves
1 egg

Preheat oven to 350°. Blend bacon drippings, molasses, and sugar. Sift together flour, salt, baking soda, and spices. Stir a small amount of flour mixture into molasses mixture. Beat in egg. Add remaining flour, stirring until smooth. Drop by teaspoonfuls onto greased baking sheet, about 2½ inches apart. Bake about 15 minutes, or until lightly browned. Remove from baking sheets and cool on racks.

Little Will's Cookies

about 3 dozen

½ cup butter
⅓ cup sugar
½ cup molasses
2 eggs, well beaten
2 tablespoons sour milk

2½ cups sifted all-purpose flour
½ teaspoon salt
1 teaspoon baking soda
¾ teaspoon ground ginger
½ cup seedless raisins, chopped

Preheat oven to 375°. Cream together butter and sugar until light and fluffy. Stir in molasses, eggs, and milk. Beat well. Sift together flour, salt, baking soda, and ginger. Stir into creamed mixture. Stir in raisins. Drop by teaspoonfuls onto greased baking sheets. Bake 12 to 15 minutes. Remove from baking sheet and cool on wire racks.

Every Day Cookies

about 3 dozen

1 cup butter, softened
⅔ cup sugar
1 teaspoon vanilla extract or other
   flavoring

2 eggs
1½ cups sifted all-purpose flour
¼ teaspoon salt

Preheat oven to 350°. Cream together butter and sugar until light and fluffy. Add vanilla and eggs and beat well. Add flour and salt and stir until a smooth dough is formed. Drop by half-teaspoonfuls onto greased baking sheets. Bake about 10 minutes, or until edges are lightly browned. Remove from baking sheets and cool on wire racks.

VII
Beverages

Most early Americans favored strong drinks, for it was believed, as Ben Franklin said, that "Water's good neither for Body nor Mind." Beer, cider, and rum were everyday drink. Beer and cider were made at home, or at least locally, and rum was, in a roundabout fashion, a by-product of the slave trade, by way of the West Indies. Wines were made locally of an amazing variety of ingredients, some of them very off-putting, but excellent wines were imported as well, and handsome crystal decanters and glasses graced the tables of the gentry. At parties and festive gatherings all kinds of punches were enjoyed. Here are julep and flip, switchel (as near to plain water as a colonial was likely to come) and smash, to enhance every occasion.

Iced Tea Juleps   *4 servings*

3 tablespoons mint-flavored   4 ounces bourbon
   iced-tea mix   Fresh mint

Stir iced-tea mix into 2 cups water. Fill four tall glasses with crushed ice. Pour 1 ounce bourbon and ½ cup tea over ice in each glass. If necessary, add ice to fill glass. Garnish with fresh mint.

Cranberry Juice Drink   *4 to 6 servings*

1 quart cranberries, washed   Fresh herb bouquet (lemon thyme,
2 cups sugar   lemon balm, hyssop, and burnet)

Mix berries, sugar, and 2 cups boiling water and boil until berries are very soft. Put through a strainer or food mill. Add fresh herb bouquet. Boil 5 minutes longer. Remove herbs and chill before serving.

Switchel or Swizzle   *about 15 servings*

It was considered dangerous for overheated haymakers to drink large quantities of water, so the water was mixed with either raw oatmeal or a combination of molasses, vinegar, and ginger. On occasions the drink was spiked with hard cider. To 1 gallon of water, add 3 cups molasses, 1 cup vinegar, and 1 teaspoon ginger. Stir well before drinking. These proportions may be altered to suit individual tastes.

Dandelion Wine   *about 5 to 6 quarts*

New Englanders made wine from dandelions, elderberries, raspberries, beets, potatoes—in fact from anything that came readily to hand and that would ferment into a pleasant-tasting drink.

3 quarts dandelion blossoms, stems   3 lemons, sliced
   removed   1 cake yeast
3 oranges, sliced   5 pounds sugar

Pick over dandelion blossoms and remove all stems and wilted blossoms. Place in a large crock and pour 4 quarts boiling water over the blossoms. Cover and let stand 3 days, stirring occasionally each day. At end of third day, strain liquid and return it to the crock. Add oranges, lemons, yeast, and sugar. Cover and let stand 3 days, stirring at least once every day. At end of third day, strain liquid and return it to the crock. Let stand in crock, covered, 4 weeks, in a moderately cool place; do not chill. At the end of 4 weeks, strain, bottle in sterilized bottles, and cap.

Mulled Apple Cider

6 servings

4 cups sweet apple cider
½ cup firmly packed brown sugar
Juice of 1 lemon
6 whole cloves

1-inch piece stick cinnamon
¼ teaspoon ground nutmeg
¼ teaspoon ground ginger
1 orange, sliced

Combine all ingredients except orange slices in a saucepan. Place over low heat and bring just to the boiling point. Stir well and serve piping hot with a slice of orange in each cup.

Apple Toddy

12 servings

24 large cooking apples
2 quarts apple brandy
¼ cup firmly packed brown sugar
¼ cup ground ginger

12 whole cloves
2 tablespoons ground cinnamon
1 teaspoon ground nutmeg

Preheat oven to 350°. Core but do not peel 12 of the apples. Place in a roasting pan and bake 45 minutes to 1 hour, or until skins burst and apples become very soft. Remove from oven and mash in the pan. Add apple brandy and blend well. Stir in brown sugar and ginger. Pour mixture into large jars, seal tightly, and store at least 24 hours before using. To serve, preheat oven to 350°. Core and peel remaining apples. Stud each one with a clove and dust tops with cinnamon. Bake 35 to 45 minutes, or just until tender; do not overcook. Put the toddy mixture from the sealed jars into a punch bowl. Stir in 6 cups boiling water. Float apples in mixture and serve each cup with a dash of nutmeg.

New England Toddy

1 serving

In a medium-sized tumbler or mug dissolve 1 teaspoon of sugar in a little boiling water. Add 1 ounce applejack and half a small baked apple. Fill glass about two-thirds full with boiling water. Stir well and sprinkle with nutmeg. Serve with a spoon.

Hot Whiskey Toddy

1 serving

Fill a glass half full with boiling water. Add 1 lump of sugar and stir well to dissolve. Add 1 jigger whiskey and a twist of lemon peel. Stir. Serve piping hot.

Southern Toddy

1 serving

In a glass, dissolve 1 lump of sugar in a little water. Stir well. Stir in 1 jigger bourbon and a twist of lemon peel. Add ice cubes and stir well.

Syllabub

Syllabub is closely related to eggnog, although eggnog calls for strong liquor and syllabub traditionally has been made with wine, making it what many think of as a ladies' drink. Traditionally it is a Christmas drink, served with cookies, and is mild enough for children. However, as with many other recipes, there are many versions. There is a thick syllabub that is served in dishes as a dessert and a thinner version served as a drink. An old recipe says: "Fill a bowl with wine and place under a cow and then milk the cow into the bowl until a fine froth has formed at the top." A second: "Sweeten a quart of cyder with refined sugar and a grating of nutmeg, then milk your cow into your liquor until you have the amount you consider proper, then top it off with about a half a pint of the sweetest, thickest cream." There are recipes for syllabubs made with wine and topped with a froth of whipped egg white and syllabubs made with wine and brandy and topped with a froth of whipped cream. Over either of these froth toppings, nutmeg was often sprinkled. The Whipt Syllabub recipe given on the following page is for a thick concoction and was usually served as dessert, along with cookies or cake.

Mint Julep
1 serving

Crush 2 or 3 mint leaves with 2 or 3 teaspoons sugar syrup in a chilled silver julep cup or chilled cut-glass goblet. Fill the julep cup with dry crushed ice. (Ice should be crushed and rolled in a linen towel so that it will be dry, not wet and mushy.) Pour in 2 jiggers bourbon. Stir with a long spoon, being careful not to touch the cup with the spoon. Stir until cup becomes frosty. Put sprigs of mint in top of cup and serve immediately.

Note: *Depending on the part of the country or the state of mind, variations on a Mint Julep are many; whether the mint should be bruised with the sugar and water, or whether it should remain untouched, is one bone of contention. The kind of liquor to use is another, varying from bourbon in Kentucky to rum, rye, and a combination of brandy and peach brandy in other julep-relishing parts of the country.*

Southern Wassail
about 50 servings

1 gallon apple cider	2 cups sugar
48 whole cloves	1 cup orange juice
1 tablespoon whole allspice	6 tablespoons lemon juice
6 small pieces stick cinnamon	4 cups apple brandy

Combine apple cider, cloves, allspice, cinnamon, sugar, orange juice, and lemon juice in a large saucepan. Bring to a boil slowly and simmer 10 minutes. Strain into another saucepan. Add apple brandy and heat, but do not boil. Serve hot in punch cups.

A Whipt Syllabub.

Take two porringers of cream and one of white wine, grate in the ſkin of a lemon, take the whites of three eggs, ſweeten it to your taſte, then whip it with a whiſk, take off the froth as it riſes and put it into your ſyllabub glaſſ- es or pots, and they are fit for uſe.

A Whipt Syllabub   *15 servings*

2 cups white wine   *3 cups milk*
Grated peel of 1 lemon   *2 cups heavy cream*
Sugar   *3 egg whites*

Combine wine, lemon peel, and 1 cup sugar. Stir to dissolve sugar. Add milk and cream. Beat with a rotary beater until mixture is frothy. Beat egg whites until stiff. Gradually add 6 tablespoons sugar, beating constantly until mixture forms stiff peaks. Pour wine mixture into a chilled punch bowl. Top with spoonfuls of egg white. Serve some white on top of each glass of syllabub.

Hot Buttered Rum　　　　　　　　　　　　　　　　　*1 serving*

In a heated medium-sized tumbler or mug dissolve 1 teaspoon brown sugar with a little boiling water. Add 1½ ounces rum and 1 tablespoon butter. Fill tumbler with boiling water. Stir well and serve with a grating of nutmeg or a cinnamon stick.

Note: *A more flavorful drink is made with hot apple cider in place of boiling water. Hot buttered rum was favored on cold winter nights and was probably the most popular hot drink in New England.*

Flip　　　　　　　　　　　　　　　　　　　*6 to 8 servings*

4 egg yolks　　　　　　　　　　　　　*1 quart rich milk*
4 teaspoons sugar　　　　　　　　　　*4 jiggers whiskey*
¼ teaspoon grated nutmeg

Beat egg yolks, sugar, and nutmeg with a rotary beater until thick and light in color. Beat in milk and whiskey. Add 1 cup crushed ice and stir until well chilled. Strain into tall stemmed glasses. Serve with freshly grated nutmeg on each serving, if desired.

Hot Flip　　　　　　　　　　　　　　　　　　*6 servings*

4 eggs　　　　　　　　　　　　　　*½ cup dark rum*
¼ cup sugar　　　　　　　　　　　　*1 quart ale*
1 teaspoon grated nutmeg

Beat eggs and sugar together until thick and light in color. Beat in nutmeg and rum. Pour mixture into a pitcher. Heat ale and pour into another pitcher. Pour the hot ale, a little at a time, into egg mixture, stirring briskly to prevent curdling. Then pour the contents of the two pitchers back and forth until the mixture is smooth and well blended. Serve immediately with a grating of fresh nutmeg on the top, if desired.

Fish House Punch　　　　　　　　　　　　　*45 to 50 servings*

1½ cups sugar　　　　　　　　　　　*1 quart brandy*
1 quart lemon juice　　　　　　　　　*½ cup peach brandy*
2 quarts Jamaica rum

Dissolve sugar in a small amount of cold water; stir well. Stir in lemon juice. Pour mixture over a block of ice in a punch bowl. Add remaining ingredients in order listed; stir lightly. Allow mixture to stand for a few hours, stirring occasionally.

Plantation Eggnog

60 servings

5 dozen eggs, separated
4 cups sugar
1½ quarts rye whiskey

1 pint rum
1½ quarts heavy cream
½ teaspoon salt

Beat egg yolks with sugar until thick and light in color. Slowly beat in whiskey and rum. Beat egg whites until very stiff. Fold into yolk mixture. Whip cream with salt until thick. Partially fold into eggnog, leaving some cream floating on top. Serve chilled.

Southern Eggnog

25 servings

6 eggs, separated
½ cup sugar, divided
1 quart brandy

1 cup peach brandy
1 quart light cream
Grated nutmeg

Beat egg yolks with ⅓ cup sugar until very light in color. Add brandy and peach brandy slowly, beating constantly all the time. Beat egg whites until stiff peaks form. Fold two-thirds of the egg whites into egg yolk mixture, reserving one-third. Stir in cream. Add remaining sugar to remaining egg whites and beat until glossy. Float in piles on top of the eggnog mixture. Dust top with freshly grated nutmeg.

Old Salem Smash

1 serving

In a tall glass put 2 tablespoons sugar, 2 tablespoons water, and 4 sprigs fresh mint. Rub together to bring out flavor of mint. Fill glass about two-thirds full with shaved ice and add 2 ounces New England rum. Mix well.

Port Punch

20 servings

The best rums, brandies, and wines—including champagne—were available to those who could afford them in all the larger cities of the colonies. To give an entertainment of any size whose refreshments did not include one of the flavored punches was unthinkable. The celebration of a wedding and the solemnity of a funeral, as well as balls, private concerts, and all sorts of galas, were considered appropriate occasions for a "flowing bowl."

2 tablespoons sugar
1 lemon
1 orange

1 cinnamon stick
1 quart Port wine

Combine sugar with 1 quart boiling water in a saucepan. Peel the lemon and orange in spirals and add peel to mixture. Squeeze the juice of the lemon and add to mixture. Stir in cinnamon stick and Port wine. Heat about 10 minutes, but do not boil. Serve hot with a dusting of freshly grated nutmeg, if desired.

Punch-Punch

30 to 35 servings

1 pound sugar
1 quart hot, strong green tea
Juice of 12 lemons
1 pint peach brandy

1 quart dark rum
2 quarts brandy
Carbonated water

Dissolve sugar in hot tea; stir well. Add lemon juice, peach brandy, rum, and brandy. Pour over a block of ice in a punch bowl. Add 1 to 2 quarts carbonated water, according to taste. Stir lightly and serve chilled.

Strong Punch

about 20 servings

8 lemons
1½ cups sugar
1 cup brandy

½ cup peach brandy
½ cup dark rum
1 quart champagne

Squeeze the juice from the lemons. Combine in a punch bowl with the sugar, brandy, peach brandy, and rum. Stir well. Let stand 3 to 4 hours before serving. Add 1 large chunk of ice. Slowly add the champagne and serve immediately.

Rum Punch

about 20 servings

1 bottle New England rum
½ pint light rum
1 cup brandy
1 cup claret
1 cup cold strong tea

3 oranges, sliced
1 pineapple, peeled and sliced
1 cup sugar
1 bottle chilled champagne or
*   carbonated water*

Combine all ingredients except champagne and let stand overnight. Place a block of ice in a punch bowl. Pour over combined ingredients. Add champagne and stir lightly. Serve in small cups.

Service Punch

25 servings

2 quarts brandy
1 quart dark rum
1 quart peach brandy
2 cups curaçao

1 cup lemon juice
2 cups superfine sugar
Orange and lemon slices

Combine brandy, rum, peach brandy, curaçao, lemon juice, and sugar in a punch bowl. Stir until ingredients are well blended. Add a block of ice and stir lightly. Garnish with orange slices and lemon slices and serve immediately.

VIII
Relishes
and Preserves

Throughout the growing season, as the various fruits and vegetables ripened, the colonial cook was constantly mindful of the cold, lean months ahead. Stories of the early winters of privation, in some cases starvation, were still told and heeded. To lay up a store of the precious fruits and vegetables to last through the cold weather, colonial cooks devised many kinds of pickles and preserves, jams and jellies. The tang of relishes and the sweet goodness of fruit preserves are still especially welcome today when you make them yourself from fresh ingredients.

Bread and Butter Pickles

Small crisp cucumbers
8 small white onions, thinly sliced
½ cup salt
5 cups sugar
5 cups vinegar

1 teaspoon ground turmeric
½ teaspoon whole cloves
2 tablespoons mustard seed
1 teaspoon celery seed

Wash cucumbers and cut in very thin slices enough to measure 4 quarts. Place in a large bowl or pan with onion. Sprinkle with salt. Cover and weight the cover; let stand overnight. Drain liquid. Combine remaining ingredients and place in a heavy kettle with cucumbers and onion. Place over low heat and bring mixture slowly to a boil, stirring occasionally; do not allow to boil. Pour mixture into hot sterilized jars and seal.

Corn Relish

10 pints

Corn, which turned up in so many kinds of dishes at so many kinds of colonial meals, was made into a tasty relish like this one by New England and Pennsylvania Dutch housewives alike.

18 ears corn	2 teaspoons celery seed
1 head green cabbage	2 teaspoons mustard seed
4 large yellow onions	2 quarts vinegar
6 green peppers, seeded	1/4 cup salt
6 small hot red peppers	2 cups sugar

Cut corn from cobs and place in a large kettle. Cut green cabbage in sections and put through the coarse blade of a food chopper with the onion, green pepper, and hot red pepper. Add to corn in kettle. Add remaining ingredients. Bring to a boil; reduce heat and simmer about 25 minutes. Ladle into hot sterilized jars and seal immediately.

Old-Fashioned Cauliflower Pickles

5 quarts

3 large heads cauliflower	2 teaspoons celery seed
1 quart white vinegar	1 teaspoon ground turmeric
1/2 cup sugar	1/4 teaspoon whole cloves
1/2 cup dried onion flakes	1 small dried red pepper
2 1/2 teaspoons salt	1 can (4 ounces) pimiento, drained
2 teaspoons mustard seed	and cut in strips

Remove large leaves from cauliflower; break into flowerettes. (This amount should make about 6 quarts.) In a large pot bring 4 quarts of water to a boil. Add cauliflower. Cover; remove from heat and let stand. In a large saucepan combine 1 1/2 quarts water with vinegar, sugar, onion flakes, salt, mustard and celery seed, and turmeric. Tie cloves and red pepper in cheesecloth. Add to vinegar mixture. Bring to boiling point. Boil, uncovered, 5 minutes. Drain cauliflower. Pour hot vinegar mixture over cauliflower. Add pimiento. Return to boiling point and cook 3 to 5 minutes, or until cauliflower is crisp-tender. Remove spice bag. Pack into hot sterilized jars. Seal at once.

Spiced Pickled Peaches

4½ *quarts*

4 cups sugar
2 cups white vinegar
4 2-inch pieces stick cinnamon

2 teaspoons whole allspice
2 teaspoons whole cloves
5 pounds firm, ripe peaches

In a large saucepan combine sugar, vinegar, and cinnamon sticks with 1 cup water. Tie allspice and cloves in cheesecloth; add to sugar mixture. Bring to a boil; cover and simmer 5 minutes. Reserve. Fill another large saucepan with water; bring to a boil. Drop peaches into boiling water for a few seconds, drain, and cover with cold water. Slide skins off peaches. Add peaches to spiced syrup. Cover and simmer 10 to 15 minutes, or until peaches are tender. (To test for doneness, pierce with a toothpick.) Pack peaches and cinnamon into hot sterilized jars, discarding spice bag. Fill jars with hot syrup. Seal at once. Let stand 6 to 8 weeks before serving.

Crisp Watermelon Rind Pickles

7 *pints*

4½ quarts (6½ pounds) prepared
watermelon rind
2 tablespoons slaked lime
10 cups sugar
2½ cups cider vinegar

7 2-inch pieces stick cinnamon
2½ tablespoons whole cloves
2½ tablespoons whole allspice
4 1-inch pieces gingerroot

Use the rind from a firm, not overripe, watermelon. Before weighing or measuring, trim off the green skin and pink flesh. Cut into 1-inch squares to measure. Mix slaked lime with 3½ quarts cold water and pour over melon rind. Soak overnight. Drain and rinse thoroughly in cold water. Place in a large kettle and cover with cold water. Bring to a boil; lower heat and simmer 2 hours. Drain. Cover with cold water again. Bring to a boil and simmer 20 to 25 minutes. Drain. Cover with cold water a third time. Bring to a boil and simmer 25 minutes, or until tender when pierced with a toothpick. Let stand in liquid overnight. In a saucepan combine sugar with 2½ quarts water. Add vinegar and cinnamon. Tie cloves, allspice, and ginger in a square of cheesecloth. Add to mixture. Bring to a boil and boil 5 minutes. Drain watermelon rind and add to syrup. Simmer slowly, uncovered, about 1 hour or until rind is clear and the syrup is slightly thickened. Remove spice bag. Pack rind in clean, sterilized jars. Pour boiling syrup over rind. Seal at once.

Sweet Pickled Crabapples

Wash the fruit, but leave the stems on. To each pound of fruit, add ¾ pound sugar, 1 cup cider vinegar, and 1 cup water. Tie a dozen cloves, two 3-inch sticks of cinnamon, and a few blades of mace in a square of muslin. Make a syrup of the sugar, vinegar, water, and spices and simmer about 3 minutes. Add crabapples and simmer just until tender. Do not overcook. Ladle into hot sterilized jars, covering the apples with the syrup. Seal. Serve cold as a relish with any kind of meat or fowl.

Currant Catsup   *about 4 pints*

Grape, currant, gooseberry, and other kinds of catsups were used on colonial tables as we use tomato catsup today. Tomatoes were not introduced in the United States until late in the 1700s and were not entirely accepted until the middle of the 1800s. Actually, all relishes and pickles were used to enhance the flavor of the table food and also were a way of "putting by" fruits and vegetables for the winter.

5 pounds currants	*1 teaspoon salt*
3 pounds sugar	*1 teaspoon ground allspice*
1 cup vinegar	*½ teaspoon pepper*
1 teaspoon ground cloves	*Dash of red pepper*
1 teaspoon ground cinnamon	

Wash and pick over currants, removing stems and spoiled berries. Place in a pot with a small amount of water and cook until very soft. Put through a sieve, removing skins. Add remaining ingredients to pulp and boil, stirring occasionally, until mixture thickens. Pour into hot sterilized jars and seal.

Note: *All ingredients can be boiled together, without straining, if you prefer to leave skins in your catsup.*

Gooseberry Catsup   *about 5 pints*

6 pounds gooseberries	*1 teaspoon ground allspice*
4 pounds brown sugar	*½ teaspoon cayenne*
2 teaspoons ground cinnamon	*2 cups vinegar*
1 teaspoon ground cloves	

Wash and pick over gooseberries, removing all stems. Place in a kettle with a small amount of water and cook until tender. Put through a sieve. Return pulp to the kettle and add brown sugar, cinnamon, cloves, allspice, and cayenne. Bring to a boil and simmer 1 hour, stirring often. Add vinegar and simmer at least 15 minutes more, or until of desired consistency. Pour into hot sterilized jars or bottles and seal.

Grape Catsup

about 3 pints

3 quarts green or purple grapes
2 pounds brown sugar
2 cups vinegar
2 tablespoons ground cloves

2 tablespoons ground allspice
2 tablespoons ground cinnamon
1 teaspoon salt
1 teaspoon cayenne

Wash and pick over grapes; remove stems and any spoiled grapes. Place in a kettle with a small amount of water and simmer until grapes are cooked. Put through a sieve to remove skins and seeds. Return pulp to kettle and add remaining ingredients. Simmer gently, stirring often, until mixture thickens and is of desired consistency. Pour into sterilized jars and seal.

Spiced Cranberry Sauce

1¼ cups

¾ pound fresh cranberries
⅓ cup cider vinegar
¾ cup light brown sugar
¼ teaspoon ground cloves
¼ teaspoon ground ginger

¼ teaspoon paprika
½ teaspoon ground cinnamon
Pinch of salt
1 tablespoon butter

Wash cranberries and cook with vinegar and ½ cup water in a covered saucepan 5 minutes, or until soft and tender. Strain through a sieve. Add brown sugar, spices, and salt. Simmer about 3 minutes, or until the mixture begins to thicken. Stir in butter. Pour into a jar and store at room temperature. Serve with pork, turkey, duck, chicken, veal, or ham.

Spiced Apple Wedges

8 servings

2 cups sugar
¼ teaspoon salt
2 4-inch sticks cinnamon

¾ teaspoon whole cloves
1 1-inch blade mace
4 cooking apples

Combine sugar, salt, and 1½ cups water in a deep 10-inch skillet. Tie spices in a cheesecloth bag and add. Boil 2 minutes. Peel, core, and quarter apples. (If apples are very large, cut into eighths.) Add to boiling syrup. Cook, uncovered, about 10 minutes, or until tender, turning apples carefully to cook uniformly. Remove apples and cool. Reserve syrup for cooking more apples at another time. Serve apple wedges with any cut of pork or with ham.

Apple Butter   *about 6 quarts*

2 gallons apple cider
8 quarts peeled, cored, and quartered
  apples
6 cups sugar

2 tablespoons ground cinnamon
1 teaspoon ground cloves
1 teaspoon ground allspice

Let cider boil until it cooks down to half its original volume. Add apples, a quart or two at a time, and cook over low heat until apples are all cooked; this will take several hours. Add sugar and spices. Cook, stirring very often, until apple butter thickens. Be very careful that it does not burn. To test apple butter, take a spoonful out and drop on a plate. If it holds its shape, it has cooked long enough. Pour into hot sterilized jars and seal.

Blueberry Butter   *about 8 pints*

8 cups fresh blueberries
8 large green cooking apples, peeled,
  cored, and sliced
8 cups sugar

1 teaspoon ground allspice
1 teaspoon ground mace
1 teaspoon ground nutmeg

Wash blueberries in a colander. Combine with remaining ingredients in a large kettle. Bring to a boil, lower heat, and simmer 1 hour, or until mixture is very thick, stirring occasionally. Ladle mixture into hot sterilized glasses. Seal and cool. Store jars in a cool dry place.

Jelly

Making jelly today is a simple matter of using pectin and following the directions that come with the product. The early settlers had to make their jams and jellies without pectin, which in most cases meant long hours of cooking until the jelly reached the stage where it would set. However, apples naturally contain pectin, and alone or in combination they produce the fastest jams or jellies to make, cooking quickly and setting quickly. To test jelly, take a small amount in a spoon and allow to cool slightly. Then let it drop from the side of the spoon. If the drops cling together or form a sheet, the jelly is ready. Another test is to spoon a small amount into a saucer and allow it to cool. If it hardens around the edge, the jelly is ready. This is also a test for apple butter.

Apple Jelly

Wash 5 pounds tart apples and cut into quarters. Do not peel or core. Put into a large, heavy kettle. Add 5 cups cold water and simmer slowly until apples are tender. Pour mixture into a jelly bag and let drip into a pot or bowl until all the juice is out. Do not squeeze the jelly bag or the jelly will not be clear. Measure juice into a pan and add ¾ cup sugar for each cup of juice. Bring slowly to a boil and boil until the syrup sheets from a silver spoon or until proven by another jelly test. Skim and pour into hot sterilized jelly glasses. Seal with hot paraffin.

Note: *Because apple jelly is fairly bland it was often flavored with sweet herbs or mixed with other fruits. When the jelly was poured into glasses, a piece or two of a favorite herb was placed on the top before sealing. Spices such as cloves, ginger, and cinnamon were often added for flavor. Before the days of paraffin, a round of tissue paper soaked in brandy was fitted over the top of the jelly and then the cover was put on. The brandy not only flavored the jelly but acted as a preservative.*

Currant Jelly

Select currants that are ripe but not too soft. Clean well and wash; remove all stems. Mash the currants in a large, heavy kettle and add ½ cup of water for each 2 quarts of fruit. Bring to a boil, stirring occasionally to keep from burning. Boil 10 minutes. Strain mixture through a jelly bag. Let drip several hours so that all the juice is strained out, but do not squeeze the bag. Measure the juice and add ¾ cup sugar for each cup of juice. Bring slowly to a boil and make the jelly test frequently. When the mixture has jelled, pour into hot sterilized jars. Allow to cool, then cover with melted paraffin.

Variation: For a change of flavor use half currants and half raspberries.

Beach Plum Jelly

Stem and wash firm ripe plums. Place in a large heavy saucepan or kettle. Add enough water to cover the plums about halfway. Cover kettle and cook over moderate heat until the plums are very tender. Turn mixture into a jelly bag, or into a colander lined with several layers of cheesecloth that have been rinsed in water. Allow juice to drip through the cloth. Do not squeeze or mash the fruit; if necessary, let stand overnight. When all the juice has drained through, measure it into a large heavy kettle. Add 1 cup sugar for each cup of juice. Mix thoroughly and bring slowly to a boil. Reduce to simmer and cook, uncovered, until jelly reaches a temperature of 220°. Remove from heat. Pour into hot sterilized jelly glasses. When jelly has set a little, cover with a thin layer of melted paraffin. Let stand until the paraffin has solidified; then cover with a second layer of paraffin.

Note: *If a thermometer is not available, test the jelly for doneness by the sheet test, page 147.*

Black 'n' Blue Berry Jam

4 to 5 8-ounce jars

2 quarts blackberries, crushed (about
  5 cups)
1 pint blueberries

4 cups sugar
3 tablespoons lemon juice

Combine all ingredients in a deep heavy kettle. Bring slowly to a boil, stirring almost constantly. Cook over moderate heat, stirring frequently, 25 to 30 minutes, or until moderately thickened. The jam will thicken as it stands, so do not overcook. Remove from the heat and ladle immediately into hot sterilized jelly jars or glasses. Fill to within ¼ inch from the top. Cool slightly. Cover with a thin layer of melted paraffin. Let stand until paraffin has solidified; then cover with a second layer of paraffin.

Strawberry Peach Jam

about 5 8-ounce jars

1 quart coarsely chopped, peeled,
  pitted ripe peaches
1 quart sliced strawberries

6 cups sugar
2 tablespoons lemon juice

Combine peaches and ¼ cup water in a large kettle. Cover and cook gently 5 minutes. Add strawberries, cover, and cook 5 minutes longer. Add sugar and lemon juice. Stir over moderate or low heat until sugar dissolves. Bring to a boil and cook rapidly, stirring frequently, 20 to 25 minutes, or until thickened. The jam thickens as it stands, so do not overcook. Remove from heat and ladle into hot sterilized jars. Fill to within ⅛ inch of the top and seal immediately with tight caps.

Pickled Beets

about 3 quarts

3 quarts small fresh beets
2 cups sugar
2 cups cider vinegar

1 teaspoon whole cloves
1 teaspoon whole allspice
2 sticks cinnamon

Wash and drain beets. Cover with boiling water and cook about 20 minutes, or until tender. Drain well. When beets are cool, remove skins, stems, and root ends. Combine sugar, vinegar, spices, and 2 cups water in a saucepan and bring to a boil. Add cooked beets and simmer 10 minutes. Pack into hot sterilized jars; seal immediately. Process in boiling water 30 minutes.

Dilled Green Bean Pickles

about 4 pints

2 pounds fresh crisp green beans
1 tablespoon salt
4 cups cider vinegar
1 cup sugar

2 tablespoons mixed pickling spice
2 cloves garlic
Fresh or dried dill

Wash beans in cool water. Snip off tops and remove strings if necessary. Leave beans whole. Soak in ice water for 30 minutes. Add salt to 1 quart water and bring to a boil. Drain beans and add to hot brine. Simmer about 20 minutes, or until just crisply tender. Drain thoroughly. Combine vinegar and sugar in a saucepan. Tie the spice in a cheesecloth bag and add to mixture with garlic. Add beans and simmer 10 minutes. Pack beans standing upright into hot sterilized jars. Cover with hot vinegar mixture. Place a head or so of dill in top of each jar. Seal.

Pumpkin Pickles

2 to 3 pints

1 pumpkin (about 4 pounds)
2¼ cups sugar
2¼ cups cider vinegar

3 sticks cinnamon
15 whole cloves

Cut pumpkin into chunks. Scrape out the pulp and seeds and remove rind. Cut into 1-inch squares. There should be about 6 cups of prepared pumpkin. Set aside. Combine sugar, vinegar, 3 cups water, cinnamon, and cloves in a large heavy-bottomed pan. Bring to a boil and boil gently 10 minutes. Add pumpkin pieces and boil gently 5 minutes. Remove from heat, cover, and let stand 1 hour. Return to heat and boil gently, uncovered, about 1 hour, or until pieces are translucent. Turn pieces occasionally during cooking time. Pack into hot sterilized jars. Seal at once. Process 10 minutes.

Sauerkraut

about 8 quarts

20 pounds cabbage

½ pound salt

Select sound, mature heads of cabbage. Remove outer leaves and rinse cabbage with cold water. Cut heads in quarters, remove cores, and shred. Mix cabbage with salt. Pack firmly into one large or two small crocks. Cover with a clean cloth and a piece of wood, heavy enough to make the cloth absorb the brine. When fermentation or bubbling begins, remove the scum from the top of the kraut every day. Cover with a clean cloth. Wash the wood and replace on top of cloth. Let stand in a cool place, about 60°, for at least a month. When fermentation has ceased, heat the kraut to simmering, about 180°. Pack the kraut into sterilized jars, leaving ½ inch space at the top. Cover kraut with brine. Seal the jars. Process in boiling water bath 25 minutes for pints and 30 minutes for quarts.

Sweet Relish

3 pints

8 large ripe cucumbers
¼ cup salt
4 large red peppers, seeded and cored
4 large onions, quartered

1½ tablespoons celery seed
1½ tablespoons mustard seed
2½ cups sugar
1½ cups white vinegar

Peel cucumbers and cut into slices. Put in a glass bowl. Add the salt and mix well. Cover and let stand in the refrigerator overnight. Drain well. Put through food chopper with peppers and onions, using the coarse blade. Place chopped vegetables in a large kettle with remaining ingredients. Bring to a boil and cook about 30 minutes, stirring occasionally, or until mixture is thickened and vegetables are cooked. Pack mixture into hot sterilized jars. Seal at once.

Cucumber Slices

5 to 6 pints

12 large cucumbers
6 medium onions
¼ cup salt
1 quart vinegar

2 cups brown sugar
1 tablespoon dry mustard
1 tablespoon turmeric
1 tablespoon cornstarch

Wash, peel, and slice cucumbers and onions. Cover with salt and let stand overnight. Combine vinegar and sugar and bring to a boil. Mix dry mustard, turmeric, and cornstarch. Mix with a little cold vinegar or water to make a paste. Add to hot vinegar mixture and bring to a boil, stirring. Drain cucumbers and onions well. Put into vinegar mixture and bring to a boil. Pack immediately into sterilized jars. Seal at once. Process 5 minutes.

Pickled Sweet Carrots

about 4 pints

2 quarts ¾-inch carrot slices
2 cups cider vinegar
2 cups sugar

1 tablespoon whole cloves
1 tablespoon whole allspice
2 sticks cinnamon

Cook carrots in a small amount of boiling salted water about 5 minutes, or just until crisply tender. Drain. Combine vinegar, 1½ cups water, and sugar in a saucepan. Add spices, tied in a small square of cheesecloth. Bring mixture to a boil. Add carrots and let mixture stand overnight. Bring to a boil and simmer 3 minutes. Remove spices and pack carrots into hot sterilized jars. Fill to within ½ inch of top with hot syrup. Seal immediately. Process 10 minutes.

Index

157